*Bringing Friends & Family
Back Around the Table*

---

*On the cover: Chicken & Shrimp Paella.
See page 78 for how this dish encompasses the
name of this cookbook.*

BRINGING *Friends* & *Family* BACK AROUND THE TABLE

A legacy cookbook by
TERRIE KOHL

bpc

Bringing Friends and Family Back Around the Table

Copyright © 2018 by Terrie Kohl

Mention of specific companies, organizations, or authorities in this book does not imply endorsement by the author or publisher, nor does mention of specific companies, organizations, or authorities imply that they endorse this book, its author, or the publisher.

Reproduction or other use, in whole or in part, of the contents without permission of the publisher is strictly prohibited.

Cover and book design by Holly Norian

Front cover photography by Jose Calderon

ISBN-13: 978-1-950790-11-1

Library of Congress Cataloging-in-Publication Data is on file with the publisher.

Business Publications Corporation Inc., Des Moines, IA

Business Publications Corporation Inc.
The Depot at Fourth
100 4th Street
Des Moines, Iowa 50309
(515) 288-3336

This cookbook is being dedicated to my idol and inspiration Jean Carroll Hofferber-Kohl, also known as my dear and loving Mother, without whom none of this would be possible.

From the first magic moments in her wonderful kitchen in our home in Cedar Rapids, through a lifetime of love and devotion...with all my love, Mom.

Your adoring daughter,
Terrie

Thank You

Diane and Ralph Haskins, former owners of Ador Kitchen and Baths, for their faith in me and collaborating in cooking classes in their world-class demonstration kitchen.

Cinnamon Rost of 1809 Design who has supported me from the beginning in being spot-on with all of my requests for graphics.

Mary Anne Kennedy of Primary Source who has supported me from the beginning with promotional products.

Julianna Hale for proof reading ALL of my recipes.

Thank you Ashley Bohnenkamp (publisher, WriteBrain), Barbara Hall (editor, WordsWorks), Holly Norian (layout artist, Fancy Fox), and Eve Morey Christiansen (indexer, Eve's Indexing) for making this dream a reality.

And not to be forgotten, "The Poker Girls."
(See their sweet notes on page xv)

And thank YOU. This book is not about me, this is about all of you who have supported me throughout the years and dreamed this dream with me.

contents

MY GOD-DRIVEN JOURNEY	viii
breakfast	17
appetizers	21
salads	33
soups	53
sides	65
pastas & rice dishes	79
meaty mains	97
fish & seafood mains	121
sauces & spreads	131
desserts	147
mom's recipe collection	167
grandma hofferber's recipes	195
grandma kohl's recipes	207
index	212

MY GOD-DRIVEN JOURNEY

EARLY DAYS

I grew up in Cedar Rapids, Iowa, in the 1960s, and my interest in the culinary arts began there, early in life. It all started with mud pies with phlox petals for garnish when I was a little girl. My mom, Jean Kohl, stayed at home until I was in junior high school, which gave me the opportunity to learn, every day, from the best. She was always experimenting and never made the same thing the same way twice. I sat on the countertop and had an aerial view of how she navigated the kitchen...from stove to sink, refrigerator to stove, sink to refrigerator, and her chop-chop on a butcher block cutting board that pulled out like a drawer.

My dad, Ramon Kohl, was also an influence, but in a different way. He owned a 21st Century Real Estate franchise and would regularly have the agents and their spouses over to the house. The ice crusher was in constant motion for daiquiris and pink squirrels with Mom making tasty appetizers. Mom would have bridge club, buying the tallies and the matching napkins, and of course, made more tasty morsels. The ladies would be laughing and talking, and they'd smell good. Those were the times that, for the children, it was 'come say hi and then be gone.'

Dad was a cook in the army.

One of my fondest childhood memories is of the fruits of the family backyard. We had an apple tree that had somehow been grafted with five types of apples. Dad would make apple fritters and oh, I wish I had that recipe...sprinkled with powdered sugar and drizzled with syrup, yum!

Our backyard was also blessed with a grape vine. Dad would make delicious wine in the basement with the crocks and the balloons on top to catch the gas. Mom would make jelly, with the sieve and the paraffin, the whole thing. Her grape jelly is still the best I've ever had.

When I got older, Mom started working one night a week. Those nights, she would have me cook for my dad. She would

Bringing Friends & Family Back Around the Table

set everything up for me, then I'd execute it. Dad was a good eater. He ate anything. It was a nice bonding time for us. I'm a daddy's girl. I've always felt, when daddies get baby girls, they should be prepared: It's a special time all your life.

When I was a child, restaurant occasions were rare, and usually a celebration of some sort. One of my most nostalgic restaurant dishes is batter-fried butterfly shrimp with cocktail sauce. That was the craze! I remember several restaurants in the Cedar Rapids area, including the Ced Rel and the Flame Room, that would bring out a pedestal with pickled herring, cheeses and crackers. That's where us kids were taught etiquette and manners. I tried to emulate my parents.

The table manners we learned, not just at restaurants but at home, too, included everyone sitting down at the same time, saying "please pass" and "may I be excused." We divvied up clearing the table and loading and unloading the dishwasher. We were given responsibilities. I think those things carry to my business today.

While I wasn't yet thinking of making cooking into a career, I carried my culinary interest into my college years. I loved planning events and menus as Social Chairman for my Alpha Phi sorority at the University of Northern Iowa. I studied social work and psychology. I remember the peer pressure when I was growing up, and I wanted to be able to help children.

Me, dad, and his dog Daffy, 2014.

introduction

LAUNCHED

Fast forward, I moved back home to Cedar Rapids, where a friend who owned the Sheraton Hotel introduced me to the world of hospitality. I worked at the front desk, in the dining room, and as a catering server. I watched the chef place his orders with a food distributor representative, which prompted me to pursue food brokerage as a career. I was treading water and decided it was time to forge a life path.

It was then God entered my life, and I began the God-driven journey to where I am today, unbeknownst to me. I moved to West Des Moines not knowing anyone. It was a huge risk. But I found success as a food service food broker, and I later transitioned into a food buyer position with Sysco Food Services of Iowa.

In West Des Moines, my social life began to revolve around a group of friends called "The Poker Girls." We would get together once a month, eat, drink, laugh, and play poker. When it was my turn to host, I would do research and pick a theme. I would make mudslide pie for New Orleans, things like that. The girls were always fired up when they were coming to my house. Pretty soon they started telling me I should do this for a living. I credit this group for catapulting me onto my culinary journey.

I thought, 'huh, I would need culinary school credentials…' On a work trip to the National Restaurant Association Show in Chicago, I came around the bend of an aisle and there was the New England Culinary Institute booth. Between that chance encounter and the fond memory of being in Vermont with my family when I was a little girl, I knew I was being called back to Vermont to attend that school. When I packed up my car and moved out there, I said 'move over, Julia.'"

My first day in white coat and black-and-white checkered pants, with my instant-read thermometer tucked in my coat.

Bringing Friends & Family Back Around the Table

What attracted me to NECI was the 7-to-1 ratio called a "block." Once I started classes, I was placed in a group of seven students with an instructor. We went through each course together. We were a tight group and got to know each other well. One student was impeached, so then we were down to six, and eventually we dropped down to five people, so it was an even more intimate experience between classmates and instructors alike. But that also meant we had to work extra hard, as we were assigned the same amount of work as a seven-person block.

The first six months of school was sort of like the liberal arts education of cooking: knife skills, herbs and spices, and food history. The second six months was internship. It was during this year of intensive training that I realized I was not going to be a line cook. I'm more methodic. I knew then that I wanted to be a caterer and teacher. I had this desire to teach and to share my knowledge.

While at the Institute, I was awarded several scholarships including the Educational Foundation of the National Restaurant Association Undergraduate Scholarship, finalist for the James Beard Foundation scholarship, and the prestigious Les Dames d'Escoffier International, Boston Chapter. For Les Dames, I was flown to Boston to receive my award from Julia Child herself. Move over, indeed! It was a dream come true to meet Julia. She was so lovely and had a magical aura about her. I call experiences such as these "God winks," little nudges that tell me I'm in the right place and that I'm being called to serve others.

Julia Child, her assistant, and me at the scholarship ceremony in the summer of 1997 in Boston at the Weston Copley Square

My scholarships helped me land some impressive internships during the second six-month stint of my education: The Montauk Yacht Club in Montauk, Long Island; Thyme & Again Catering; and South Hampton Bath and Tennis Club, also in Long Island. The last six months at NECI were hands-on skills: meat fabrication, garde manger, a la carte, pastry, etc. Then to

introduction

finish the culinary program, I came home to West Des Moines and interned at the Downtown Marriott Hotel, Embassy Club at Capital Square, and Aramark/Pioneer Hi-Bred. I also served as catering chef at Drake University.

These were great experiences, and great training for what I ended up offering through my business, Country Club Market: customized catering and demonstration/hands-on cooking classes. I got my wings teaching classes out of Walnut Hills United Methodist Church. I got a feel for the business and knew I could do it. I had originally envisioned having a brick-and-mortar location for teaching classes and doing catering. I had all the players. I was going to hire interns from Des Moines Area Community College (DMACC) and local mothers who would love to work in four-hour stints. I was going to do packaged meals, where people would call and say 'oh, I want that for eight.' I knew the music I would play, the location, the floor plan. I could smell it. But it was too late. By the time I was ready to take that step, the market was saturated. God told me, 'no, you're doing fine where you are.' I've been a one-woman army ever since. I eventually moved my business from the church to my home, and this year, 2018, marks my 15th anniversary as a customized caterer, culinary instructor, baker, and personal chef.

My scholarship award plaque from Les Dames d'Escoffier, handed to me by Julia Child at the ceremony.

THE JOURNEY COMPLETE

I built my home in Clive in 2001, designing it to accommodate Country Club Market to conduct my cooking classes, market bakery, and customized catering. And of course, I designed room for my cookbooks. Did I mention I'm an addict? I have 4500 + cookbooks in my collection!

Now I'm glad that I don't have a store because this is my home, and my clients feel that. They sit around my table on mismatched chairs. People come into my house as strangers, and two hours later I'm getting hugs and a 'thank you.' I'm so blessed. I say, "Thank you, God. I'm doing good work here."

At each of my classes, everyone gets a recipe packet, a full meal, and entertainment/lessons. Many times, my class members have sat around the table, held hands, and prayed. That makes me feel good. Those are the times when I know for certain this is where I'm supposed to be. I just want to de-mystify the cooking process for people.

Most of my classes are 12-15 people at a time. Any class over 20 people I hold off-site at a community kitchen. One of my favorite types of class to teach is corporate team building events. Wells Fargo brought in 15 people from around the country. They cooked together, brought wine, and played games in my backyard. They liked the homey atmosphere. Another time I had 350 Farm Bureau employees in a banquet hall at the West Des Moines Marriott. I taught the class and then the hotel kitchen staff brought out the meal.

The thing I said after, "Move over, Julia," was, "Move over, Martha." I did cooking segments with KCCI TV in Des Moines for many years. Lots of times they came and shot in my kitchen or at my grill or deck. I've also done many things with IPTV and Iowa Ingredient. This was my 19th year of judging food at the Iowa State Fair. I was also recently on a panel of three judges for the Iowa edition of the Great British Baking Show, at IPTV.

Because I feel so blessed, I take time to give back to my community. Through Lutheran Church of Hope, I discovered an opportunity with Wildwood Hills Ranch near Winterset where children in difficult family situations go for camp. I teach cooking life skills to the outreach youth. It's kind of ironic that I have come back to my original career path at UNI – social work and psychology – through my work at Wildwood Hills. All of a sudden it occurred to me that here I am giving guidance to youth through my gift of cooking. What a blessing that it came full circle!

Some of these kids are already chefs in their own right; they have to cook for their siblings. Then there are others who have no idea what goes on in a kitchen. The first time I taught, we just went through the pantry and pulled out things we could do something with: cake mix, apples, caramel. It was so fun to see their surprise that they could do a few things and it would taste so good.

So here I am, celebrating 15 years doing what I love. To celebrate, I hosted a celebratory party at Blue Moon Piano Bar in West Des Moines, I'm publishing this book, and I'm dreaming more big dreams for the next chapter of my life.

Thank you all!
Terrie

"The Poker Girls" at Vicki's annual Girls Christmas Party in 2017.
(L-R): Susan, Chris, Me, Bev, Yo, and Vicki.

Notes from "The Poker Girls"

Terrie's heart and soul are intertwined with food. She puts her whole self into the planning and preparing of food! Terrie's happy place is when she's serving her delicious dishes!

- Vicki Berberich

Terrie, I knew you would be a big success. I believe I was one of your early catering jobs, remember the chocolate covered cherries in the homemade bags and the little cakes for each table at my wedding?

- Chris Manfull-Doran

Terrie, I am just so happy you chose to follow your dream. I feel blessed to have been one of you first clients and I hope you continue to share your yummy dishes with the poker girls! Love you!

- Susan Bump

I'm happy for Terrie to be sharing part of herself with this cookbook. I have a funny story that still makes me laugh today. Terrie catered my husband's 50th birthday party (19 years ago). Of course, Terrie went all out with the food and the presentation and it was a huge hit. We were refilling dishes when we both noticed the adorable penguin garnishments she had prepared were gone (note: I love penguins). Terrie and I looked at each other and laughed because we both said, "Can you believe someone ate them?!" I love it when dreams come true. Congrats Terrie.

- Yo Holtz

introduction

The pineapple logo is the international symbol of friendship and hospitality. It is my hope that with this cookbook, you will make both food and friends.

breakfast

18   OUT OF THIS WORLD BEEF TENDERLOIN EGGS BENEDICT

19   SUMMERTIME FRESH ASPARAGUS QUICHE

OUT OF THIS WORLD BEEF TENDERLOIN EGGS BENEDICT

Four 3 to 4 oz beef tenderloin steaks

Salt and pepper

1 T olive oil

2 Bagels, sliced, Texas toast, or English muffins

4 slices fresh mozzarella

4 whole roasted red peppers

4 eggs

1 T white vinegar

1 recipe Hollandaise Sauce (page 132)

I love eggs benedict and so I took it a step up. Instead of English muffin, Canadian bacon, egg, and sauce, I use the muffin, a thin slice of beef tenderloin medallion, and seal it with roasted red pepper and sliced mozzarella.

Preheat oven to 300°F.

Season beef with salt and pepper. Heat oil in a large ovensafe skillet over high heat. When the skillet is "ripping hot", sear both sides of beef until browned. Move skillet to oven and bake until an instant-read thermometer inserted in through the side reads 145°F.

Toast bread. Have mozzarella and peppers ready.

In a large skillet, bring 4 cups of water and the vinegar to a boil. Reduce heat to a gentle simmer. Crack an egg into a small ramekin. Holding close to the surface of the water, gently slip egg into the water. Repeat with the remaining eggs, giving them an equal amount of space. Simmer 3 to 5 minutes or until whites are set and yolks are just thickened. Remove from water with a slotted spoon. Transfer to a paper towel-lined plate. Season with salt and pepper. Keep warm.

To compile, layer bread, steak, mozzarella, egg, then pepper. Drizzle with Hollandaise Sauce.

Serves 4 but can easily be adjusted for number of people

SUMMERTIME FRESH ASPARAGUS QUICHE

12 fresh asparagus spears

3 eggs

½ c skim milk

½ c heavy cream

⅓ c fresh chives, snipped

⅓ c fresh flat leaf Italian parsley, coarsley chopped

1 sheet pie crust to fit 8 or 9-inch pan

½ c havarti cheese, shredded
Lemon wedges

Preheat oven to 400°F. Line sheet pan with parchment paper.

Cut asparagus to about 4 inches to nicely fit in spiral fashion in an 8 to 9-inch springform pan. Steam 3 minutes in a perforated pan over boiling water with lid on. Then plunge immediately in ice water to stop the cooking process. Drain and blot dry with paper towels. Set aside.

Place pie crust inside springform pan, pressing into sides and bottom.

In a large bowl, whisk together eggs, milk, cream, chives, and parsley. Pour mixture into crust. Sprinkle cheese over the top. Place asparagus spears in a spoke fashion with tips out.

Place on sheet pan and bake for 30 to 40 minutes or until a knife inserted near the center comes out clean. Allow to cool briefly, 15 minutes or so. It should not jiggle.

Run a knife around the edge to release from rim, remove, and cut into wedges.

Sprinkle with a little more parsley for garnish and serve with fresh lemon wedges.

When my Grandma Kohl passed, what I really wanted was her "recipe drawer." As I was combing through the many treasured handwritten recipes in that drawer, I came across a special surprise...a construction paper Christmas card I had made for her years and years ago when I was in elementary school. How precious that she kept it all this time! I will continue to keep it with her recipe collection.

appetizers

22   SPINACH ARTICHOKE DIP

23   CAJUN APPETIZER MEATBALLS WITH ANDOUILLE SAUSAGE

24   CREAMY CRAB RANGOON DIP WITH BAKED WON-TON CHIPS

25   CURRIED COCONUT CHICKEN WINGS

26   DEVILED EGGS ITALIA

27   GRILLED SIDE OF FRESH SALMON WITH MUSTARD DILL GLAZE

28   PORK POTSTICKERS

29   RUSTIC ITALIAN TURKEY MEATBALLS

30   LUSCIOUS CRAB CAKES WITH REMOULADE SAUCE

31   PEANUT CHICKEN SATAY

SPINACH ARTICHOKE DIP

GROUP 1

8 oz package cream cheese; room temperature

8 oz Monterey Jack Cheese, shredded

1 c sour cream

½ c Parmesan Cheese, grated

¼ c dried minced onion

Chopped garlic to taste (I use 2 Tbsp)

GROUP 2

12 oz fresh spinach, uncut

14 oz can artichoke hearts, drained, whole

Chips and/or vegetable dippers

Preheat oven to 350°F.

Combine first group of ingredients, then add second group briefly.

Bake for 30 minutes or until heated through.

Serve hot with favorite chips and/or vegetables.

CAJUN APPETIZER MEATBALLS WITH ANDOUILLE SAUSAGE

1 egg, lightly beaten

½ c milk

¼ c oatmeal

1 lb hamburger

¼ c finely chopped onion (I like to use the green of a scallion)

1 T dried parsley (or ¼ c fresh chopped Italian flat leaf parsley)

2 T Cajun seasoning

1 T Worcestershire sauce

1½ t hot pepper sauce

½ c barbecue sauce

½ c raspberry jam, or any jelly/preserves

1 lb Andouille sausage, cut diagonally

Preheat oven to 350°F. Line a baking sheet with parchment paper.

In a large bowl, mix thoroughly the egg, milk, and oatmeal. This is your binding mixture. Let sit for 1 minute for oats to start softening.

Add the hamburger, onion, parsley, Cajun seasoning, Worcestershire sauce, and hot pepper sauce.

Form the mixture into golf ball-sized meatballs (I use a small ice cream scoop) and place on the baking sheet.

Bake for 30 to 40 minutes, until there is no pink left in the middle – or until an instant read thermometer reads 165°F.

Meanwhile, in a large saucepan combine and heat the barbeque sauce and jam on medium high.

Though Andouille sausage is already cooked, for additional color and flavor, heat a medium to large skillet on high, add two tablespoons of olive oil, and brown each side of the sausage slices. Set aside.

When meatballs are done, place them and the sausage in the barbeque sauce mixture.

Toss to coat, reheat if necessary, and serve hot.

These could attractively be served in a chafing dish or slow cooker.

CREAMY CRAB RANGOON DIP WITH BAKED WON-TON CHIPS

WON-TON CHIPS

14 oz package won-ton skins

¼ c liquid egg (1 beaten egg or Eggbeaters®)

¼ c milk

Sesame seeds

SWEET AND SOUR SAUCE

10 oz jar orange marmalade

⅓ c water

3 T ketchup

1 T cider vinegar

1 t fresh grated ginger

CRAB RANGOON DIP

Two 8 oz packages cream cheese, softened

2 T sugar

1 T snipped fresh chives

1 T garlic

½ t salt

1 lb lump crab meat, broken up

Milk or cream (optional)

This is a way to have this delicious treat fryer-free. The secret to a good crab Rangoon? Sugar. Asian cooking hits all the notes – sour, sweet, hot. Sugar adds a balance to the intensity of the other flavors.

Preheat oven to 350°F. Line two sheet pans with parchment paper.

Cut won-ton skins diagonally using a pizza cutter or scissors. Lay out on prepared sheet pans. In a small bowl combine egg with milk and brush over skins. Sprinkle with sesame seeds. Bake 20 minutes or until golden brown.

In a small saucepan, mix all ingredients for the sweet and sour sauce and bring to a boil, then let cool.

To make the dip, pulse cream cheese in a food processor until fluffy.

Add the sugar, chives, garlic, and salt. Pulse briefly to combine.

Lightly stir in crab meat. Adjust seasoning with additional salt, if needed. Thin to desired consistency with milk or cream.

Pour into a small oven-safe dish and bake at 350° for 20 to 30 minutes until heated through.

Serve warm with the chips and sauce in separate bowls.

CURRIED COCONUT CHICKEN WINGS

12 (2½ lb) chicken wings

1 c canned unsweetened coconut milk

1½ c panko bread crumbs

3 T shredded coconut

4 t curry powder

6 T butter, melted

2 cloves garlic, minced

Preheat oven to 375°F. Grease a 15x10x1-inch baking pan.

Cut off and discard tips of chicken wings. Cut wings at joints to form 24 pieces.

In a large bowl, pour coconut milk over wing portions. Cover and chill in the refrigerator 2 to 24 hours.

In a shallow dish, combine bread crumbs, shredded coconut, and curry powder. Dredge each wing portion in the crumb mixture and place in the prepared pan.

Combine butter and garlic. Drizzle over the wings.

Bake uncovered for 45 minutes or until well browned.

Serve hot or cold.

DEVILED EGGS ITALIA

- 1 dozen hard boiled eggs, peeled, halved lengthwise and yolks removed
- 6 canned or jarred artichoke hearts
- ¼ c chopped fresh basil
- ¼ c chopped roasted red pepper
- 3 T mayonnaise
- 2 T grated or shredded Parmesan cheese
- Salt and pepper
- Italian flat leaf parsley, coarsely chopped (optional)

This recipe was created and demonstrated for the Iowa Egg Council at their annual food competition.

In a food processor, combine egg yolks, artichoke hearts, basil, roasted red pepper, mayonnaise, and Parmesan cheese. Pulse until just blended. Season to taste with salt and pepper.

Place mixture in piping bag or Ziploc® bag with a corner snipped off. Pipe filling into egg white halves.

Garnish with parsley.

GRILLED SIDE OF FRESH SALMON WITH MUSTARD DILL GLAZE

2 T black mustard seeds

½ c mayonnaise

½ c whole-grain mustard

2 T finely chopped fresh dill

1 T fresh lime juice

1 T dark brown sugar

1 t ground black pepper

One 2-lb side of salmon, skin on

Olive oil

Salt and pepper

Nonstick cooking spray

This is one of my all-time favorites – a real impressive winner as appetizer or entrée.

Preheat an outdoor grill.

In a 7-inch dry pan, toast mustard seeds over medium heat for 2 minutes or until fragrant and they begin to pop. Transfer to a plate.

In a small bowl, whisk together mayonnaise, whole-grain mustard, dill, lime juice, brown sugar, and pepper. Set aside half of the mixture for serving.

Rub your hand over the salmon to check for pin bones. Use a tweezer to remove if you find any.

Rub olive oil over entire salmon and generously season with salt and pepper. Coat grill rack with nonstick spray. Place salmon skin side up on the grill rack directly over heat. Cover and grill 2 minutes. Give a quarter turn and grill 2 minutes more. Gently turn over so fish meat is up and coat with half of the mustard glaze. Cover and grill 8 minutes more or until fish meat flakes when tested with a fork.

Place salmon on a garnished platter with remaining glaze. Serve with crackers.

Makes 12 to 16 servings

PORK POTSTICKERS

¾ c + 2 T soy sauce

2 T fresh ginger, finely chopped

2 cloves garlic, finely chopped

1 t rice vinegar

1 t sesame oil

1 lb ground pork

½ c scallions, white and green parts, thinly sliced

½ t each salt and black pepper

1 egg

2 T water

20 won-ton wrappers

2 T canola oil

For dipping sauce, combine ¾ cup soy sauce, ginger, garlic, vinegar, and sesame oil.

For filling, combine pork, scallions, 2 tablespoons soy sauce, salt, and pepper.

In a separate bowl, beat together the egg and water.

To form the pot stickers, lay wrappers on a work surface, in batches. Place a ½ tablespoon of the filling in the center of each. Avoid getting any filling on the edges of the wrapper, otherwise they will not seal properly. With a finger or pastry brush, paint the circumference of the wrappers with the egg mixture. One at a time, fold each wrapper in half to form a half-moon shape and seal by pressing between your fingers. Starting from the center, make 3 pleats along one side, working toward a corner. Repeat, working toward the other corner. Once completely sealed, gently push the potsticker down on the work surface to form a flat bottom so it stands.

Heat a large, nonstick skillet over high heat. Add the canola oil and swirl to coat the pan. When the oil is hot, add the potstickers, in batches, and cook without disturbing 3 to 4 minutes or until brown. Add about ½ cup of water and immediately cover the pan to avoid splattering. Lift the cover and make sure about 1/8 inch of water remains in the pan; add a little more if level is too low. Steam 8 to 10 minutes or until the potstickers are puffy yet firm and the water has evaporated. If the water evaporates before the potstickers are done, add more water in ¼ cup increments. If the pot stickers seem done, but water remains in the pan, drain it and return the pan to the stovetop to evaporate any remaining liquid. Continue to cook over high heat 2 to 3 minutes to allow the pot stickers to recrisp on the bottom, careful not to burn them.

Transfer the potstickers to a platter and serve with the dipping sauce in individual ramekins.

RUSTIC ITALIAN TURKEY MEATBALLS

1 large egg

¼ c skim milk

½ c oatmeal

1 lb ground turkey breast

½ c Parmesan cheese, grated (plus more for garnish)

2 scallions, green parts only, chopped

¼ c fresh Italian parsley, coarsely chopped

1 to 2 cloves garlic, minced

1 t each salt and pepper

SAUCE

½ c olive oil

5 to 10 cloves garlic, minced

1 t crushed red pepper

1 T anchovy paste

Four 14.5-oz. cans diced Italian tomatoes, drained saving 1 c juice

12 to 15 brine-cured black olives, coarsely chopped

2 T capers

⅓ c fresh Italian parsley, chopped (plus more for garnish)

Salt and pepper

People love this! I created it to be health – turkey with oatmeal as the binder instead of bread crumbs. These flavorful delights can be served as an appetizer or used on pasta.

Preheat oven to 350°F. Line a sheet pan with parchment paper.

In a medium bowl, beat together egg and milk. Add oatmeal, turkey, Parmesan, scallions, parsley, garlic, salt, and pepper. Stir lightly to combine.

Form into 1½ inch meatballs with hands or a scoop and place on prepared pan. Bake 25 to 30 minutes or until an instant-read thermometer reads 165°F.

Meanwhile, prepare the sauce. In a saucepot, heat olive oil over medium low heat. Add garlic and crushed pepper flakes. Cook 1 minute or until fragrant.

Add anchovy paste and cook 1 minute more. Add tomatoes and juice, olives, and capers. Bring to boiling. Reduce heat and simmer. Add parsley and stir. Season to taste with salt and pepper.

Serve sauce over meatballs. Garnish with parsley and Parmesan.

Makes approximately 30 meatballs

appetizers

LUSCIOUS CRAB CAKES WITH REMOULADE SAUCE

2 eggs, lightly beaten

2½ c panko crumbs

4 scallions, sliced thin, green only

¼ c lemon juice

2 T mayonnaise

2 T Dijon mustard

1 T Old Bay Seasoning

1 T parsley, chopped

1 T chives, chopped

1 t cayenne pepper

½ t each salt and pepper

½ t Worcestershire sauce

1 lb jumbo lump crabmeat

¼ c vegetable oil

REMOULADE SAUCE

1 c mayonnaise

2 T lemon juice

2 T ketchup

2 T celery, finely diced

1 T prepared horseradish

1 T dill pickle, finely diced

1 T capers, finely diced

1 T stone ground mustard

1 T fresh parsley, finely chopped

1 T hot sauce

Make this as spicy as you like with additional cayenne and hot sauce.

Preheat oven to 400°F.

In a large bowl, thoroughly combine eggs, ½ cup panko crumbs, scallions, lemon juice, mayonnaise, Dijon, Old Bay Seasoning, parsley, chives, cayenne, salt, pepper, and Worcestershire sauce. VERY gently fold in crab, leaving lumps intact.

Divide mixture into 16 portions. Place 2 cups panko crumbs in a shallow dish. Roll each portion in panko and form into small patties. Place on a baking sheet or tray.

Cover and refrigerate at least 30 minutes.

Meanwhile, in a small bowl, stir together all ingredients for the sauce and refrigerate.

In a 10 to 12-inch frying pan, heat oil on high to sear, then turn down to medium and sauté cakes 2 to 3 minutes on each side to brown, adding additional oil as needed.

Place cakes on baking sheet and bake 5 minutes or until temperature reads 160°F.

Serve with sauce.

PEANUT CHICKEN SATAY

2 t curry powder

1 t ginger, minced

1 t garlic, minced

1 t ground cumin

½ c cream of coconut (Coco López®)

1 T lime zest

½ t chili powder

1 lb chicken breast, cut into thin lengthwise strips

Wooden skewers

Fresh cilantro

1 recipe Peanut Sauce (page 142)

Heat small skillet on medium. Add curry powder, ginger, garlic, and cumin. Cook 1 minute until curry is slightly browned.

In a meduim bowl, pour cream of coconut. Add spice mixture, lime zest, and chili powder. Add chicken and marinate refrigerated for 30 minutes. Drain chicken and discard marinade.

Preheat oven to 350°F.

Spray a preheated medium high grill with nonstick spray. Grill both sides of strips until marks appear.

Skewer each strip of chicken, once through.

Place in oven on a baking sheet and bake until 160°F or no longer pink.

Serve with hot Peanut Sauce. Garnish with cilantro.

appetizers

In days of old, when men were bold, and times did a man's courage measure, Into the hands of a pirate Captain fell, a map of buried treasure.

"Ho, Ho," he said, to his daring young men, "Let us go to the Isle of Capri, where you shall dig, and dance a jig, and find gems and gold for me."

1- "Isle of Capri" – Perry Schafer
   Pirates – Tom Bassett and Junior Thaut
   "We're Pirates bold, from days of old.
   For treasure we will dig,
   And when the chest we do find
   For you we will dance a jig.
   The jewels and gold of many hues
   We will be very proud to show to you."

2 They dug around into the ground,
  Until they found the treasure
  With hands that shook, they broke the lock
  And what they saw was quite a shock
  And also quite a pleasure.
  Do dance. Open chest and lift up treasure

This is one of three pages I found in my Grandma Kohl's recipe drawer that appears to be an outline for some sort of program. Pirates on the hunt for treasure – how fun! Continued on page 52.

salads

34	CRISP GREENS WITH WATERMELON	43	SPINACH & HERB SALAD
35	HOMEMADE CAESAR & CROUTONS	44	SPRIGHTLY SALAD OF WATERCRESS & PECAN CHÈVRE MEDALLIONS
36	ITALIAN BEAN SALAD WITH CURLY ENDIVE	45	WARM ROASTED SWEET POTATO MAPLE BACON SALAD
37	MEDITERRANEAN SALAD IN AN OVEN PANCAKE	46	PROSCIUTTO & NECTARINE SALAD
38	PEAR & WALNUT SALAD	47	FESTIVE QUINOA SALAD
39	ARUGULA WITH GOAT CHEESE MEDALLIONS	48	CRISPY COD MARKET SALAD
40	ROASTED BEET SALAD	49	FALL APPLE & WALNUT SALAD WITH MAPLE BALSAMIC VINAIGRETTE
41	ROSEMARY ROASTED ROOT VEGETABLE SALAD	50	ZESTY LIME, PINEAPPLE & AVOCADO WITH BABY GREENS
42	SALAD LYONNAISE & POACHED EGG		

TERRIE'S TIDBIT

Even if I buy a package of greens that says "pre-washed" I always wash them. Washing not only gives them an extra cleaning but also rehydrates them. It's amazing how much crisper they get!

CRISP GREENS WITH WATERMELON

¼ c white balsamic vinegar

¼ c olive oil

1 T honey

½ t pepper

2 heads romaine lettuce, cut, washed, and spun or blotted dry

2 c diced watermelon

1 c crumbled feta cheese

For the dressing, in a small bowl, whisk together vinegar, olive oil, honey, and pepper. Or place ingredients in a screw-top jar, attach lid, and shake to combine.

In a large bowl, toss together romaine, watermelon, and feta. Add dressing and toss to coat.

Pour out onto a pretty platter and serve.

Makes 6 to 8 servings

HOMEMADE CAESAR & CROUTONS

HOMEMADE CROUTONS

6 slices of any flavor of bread, cut in 1-inch cubes

⅓ c olive oil

¼ c dry parsley

1 t salt

1 t granulated garlic

1 t pepper

1 t paprika

CLASSIC CAESAR DRESSING

⅔ c mayonnaise

⅓ c sour cream

1 T anchovy paste

1 lemon, juiced (2 T)

2 t minced garlic (heaping)

2 t dried minced onion

1 t Worcestershire sauce

1 t pepper

¾ c shredded Parmesan cheese

GREENS

1 to 2 heads Romaine, cut, washed, and spun dry in a salad spinner or blotted dry with paper towels

Preheat oven to 375°F.

Place bread cubes in large bowl. Add the rest of the ingredients for the croutons and use hands to coat the bread cubes.

Spread onto sheet pan and bake 20 to 25 minutes or until browned and crisp. Stir croutons and rotate pan halfway through.

For the dressing, stir together mayonnaise, sour cream, anchovy paste, lemon juice, garlic, onion, Worcestershire sauce, and pepper. Stir in cheese. Cover and chill overnight in the refrigerator.

Just before serving, in a serving bowl toss romaine with dressing and croutons. Top with additional Parmesan cheese and cracked pepper.

Makes 6 to 8 servings

ITALIAN BEAN SALAD WITH CURLY ENDIVE

SALAD

5 c curly endive, coarsely chopped, washed and spun or blotted dry

1 c shaved fennel

½ red onion, julienned

1 c grape or cherry tomatoes, halved

1 19-oz can cannellini beans, drained

½ c shredded Italian cheese blend

Zest of 1 lemon

DRESSING

½ c balsamic vinegar

½ c olive oil

¼ cup honey

Salt and pepper

In a serving bowl, arrange salad ingredients in layers.

In a small bowl, whisk together dressing ingredients, adjust salt and pepper to taste, and pour over salad. Toss to combine.

Makes 8 to 10 servings

MEDITERRANEAN SALAD IN AN OVEN PANCAKE

2 T butter

½ c all-purpose flour

2 eggs

½ c milk

1 t minced garlic

¼ t salt

¼ t Italian seasoning

2 oz baby greens, washed and spun or blotted dry

1 c (4 oz) feta cheese, crumbled

10 kalamata olives, pitted and coarsely chopped

Olive oil

Salt

Fresh black pepper

This is a dish that is sure to wow your guests!

Preheat oven to 425°F.

Place butter in 9-inch pie pan. Bake 4 minutes or until butter is melted.

In meduim bowl, beat together flour, eggs, milk, garlic, salt, and Italian seasoning. Pour into pan.

Bake 20 to 25 minutes or until sides are puffed and deep golden brown.

Meanwhile, toss together greens, cheese, and olives. Add olive oil and salt and pepper to taste.

When oven pancake is done, remove from oven and fill with salad. Cut into wedges.

Makes 6 to 8 servings

PEAR & WALNUT SALAD

½ c rice wine vinegar

¼ c vegetable oil

2 t sugar

1 t dried minced onion

¼ t ground rosemary

Salt and pepper

¾ c dried cranberries

4 c fresh cut greens, washed and spun or blotted dry

3 to 4 pears (red if possible), cored and chopped

½ c toasted walnuts, chopped

½ c crumbled feta cheese

I love red pears for their texture and color. They are also firm – they don't get soft like a Bartlett. Since the vinaigrette is sweet, I use vegetable or corn oil. Olive oil would inroduce an overpowering flavor.

For vinaigrette, in a screw-top jar combine vinegar, oil, sugar, onion, and rosemary. Attach lid and shake well until combined. Season to taste with salt and pepper. Chill until ready to serve.

Place cranberries in a microwave-safe bowl. Add enough water to cover. Microwave on high for 1 minute. Let stand to macerate until cool then drain.

In a large bowl, toss together greens, pears, walnuts, feta, and the drained cranberries.

Add vinaigrette and toss to combine. Pour out onto platter for presentation.

Makes 6 to 8 servings

ARUGULA WITH GOAT CHEESE MEDALLIONS

6 to 8 oz pomegranate juice, frozen, thawed

⅓ c canola oil

1½ T honey

1 T white wine vinegar

1 t Dijon mustard

½ c pomegranate arils

Salt and pepper

16 oz log goat cheese (chèvre), cut into 8 slices

1 c pecans, toasted and finely chopped

3 c arugula, washed and spun dry

3 c romaine, cut, washed and spun dry

Preheat oven to 200°F. Line a sheet pan with parchment paper.

In a small bowl, whisk together pomegranate juice, oil, honey, vinegar, and mustard. Stir in pomegranate arils and season to taste with salt and pepper.

Press goat cheese slices lightly in pecans to coat. Place on parchment lined sheet pan, bake 5 minutes or until warm.

In a large bowl toss together arugula, romaine, and vinaigrette. Serve topped with warm goat cheese medallions.

Makes 6 to 8 servings

ROASTED BEET SALAD

6 beets, trimmed and washed

6 T olive oil

2 T shallots, minced

2 T white wine vinegar

1 T whole-grain mustard

½ t dried thyme

Salt and pepper

4 c mixed greens

1 c (4 oz) blue cheese crumbles

½ c toasted walnuts, chopped

¼ c coarsely chopped fresh parsley

When I roast beets I leave the skins on. Don't poke them. You want them to steam so the skin will fall right off.

Preheat oven to 400°F

Wrap beets individually in foil. Bake 1 hour or until tender, let cool in foil then remove. Gently rub with paper towel to slide off the skins. Dice, chop, or slice beets to desired size.

Whisk together olive oil, shallots, vinegar, mustard, and thyme. Season to taste with salt and pepper.

In a large bowl, toss together greens, cheese, walnuts, and parsley.

In a separate bowl, toss the beets with a small amount of the vinaigrette. Add remaining vinaigrette to the salad ingredients and toss to coat.

To serve, arrange salad on plate or in bowl and top with beets.

Makes 4 to 6 servings

ROSEMARY ROASTED ROOT VEGETABLE SALAD

SALAD

1 lb red skinned potatoes, skin on, scrubbed and cut in 1-inch pieces

1 lb sweet potatoes, skin on, scrubbed and cut in 1-inch pieces

1 lb carrots, skin on, scrubbed and cut in 1-inch pieces

1 lb red onion (skin off) scrubbed and cut in 1-inch pieces

⅓ c olive oil

2 t granulated garlic

1½ t ground dried rosemary

1½ t kosher salt

1½ t coarse ground black pepper

1 lb. beets, skin on, scrubbed and cut in 1-inch pieces

VINAIGRETTE

½ c red wine vinegar

⅓ c grated parmesan cheese

¼ c olive oil

2 T Dijon mustard

Salt and pepper

I leave the skin on vegetables for most of my recipes. It saves a step, you get more yield, and it's the healthiest part of the vegetable. Plus, you already paid for it!

Preheat oven to 425°F.

Place red and sweet potatoes, carrots, and onion in a large bowl. Toss with olive oil, garlic, rosemary, salt, and pepper. Pour onto sheet pan.

Place beets in the empty bowl and toss in residual olive oil and seasonings.

Pour out onto separate sheet pan so as not to "bleed" onto other vegetables.

Roast vegetables for 40 minutes, or until golden crispy and tender, stirring halfway through.

Whisk together all ingredients for vinaigrette.

Combine all roasted vegetables in a bowl and toss with vinaigrette.

Transfer onto a platter to serve.

Makes 6 to 8 servings

SALAD LYONNAISE & POACHED EGG

8 slices of slab bacon, cut into strips

1 large shallot, minced

2 to 3 cloves garlic, thinly sliced

¼ c olive oil

¼ c Dijon mustard

¼ c white wine vinegar

1 T fresh tarragon, chopped

Salt and pepper

10 oz mixed greens, cut, rinsed and spun or blotted dry

6 eggs

Fresh parsley, chopped

Here's a secret: poached eggs can be done in advance. That's how a lot of restaurants do it. Poach them and then hold overnight in ice water. When it's time, lift them out with a slotted spoon, submerge briefly in hot water, blot, and serve.

In a large skillet, fry bacon over medium heat until nicely browned. Remove and drain bacon on paper towels.

Leave bacon grease in the skillet and add shallot and garlic. Cook, stirring briefly, until tender.

Turn off heat and quickly stir in oil, mustard, and vinegar. May need to add small amount of hot water for desired consistency. Add tarragon and season to taste with salt and pepper. Toss with the salad greens.

Wipe out skillet and bring 4 cups of water to a boil then reduce heat to a simmer. Crack one of the eggs into a small dish and holding close to the water, slip the egg into the water. Repeat with remaining eggs. Simmer 3 minutes or until whites are set and yolks are thickened. Remove from skillet with a slotted spoon. Drain on paper towels to blot excess water. Season with salt and pepper.

To serve, top salad with eggs and bacon. Garnish with fresh parsley.

Makes 6 servings

SPINACH & HERB SALAD

5 to 6 oz fresh spinach, stems removed, rinsed, spun dry and kept cold

¼ c each of desired fresh herbs: dill, tarragon, basil, and thyme, snipped

4 strips thick sliced pepper bacon, sliced in 1-inch pieces

3 T balsamic vinegar

2 T coarse ground mustard

1 T minced garlic

Salt and pepper

6 hard boiled eggs, shelled and chopped

1 c thawed frozen peas

On a platter, combine spinach and herbs.

In a large skillet, cook bacon over medium heat until crisp. Remove from skillet and drain on paper towels.

Add vinegar, mustard, and garlic to the bacon drippings in the skillet. Whisk to combine. Season to taste with salt and pepper. Toss dressing with salad and add bacon. Top with eggs and peas.

Makes 6 to 8 servings

TERRIE'S TIDBIT

When you bring your fresh herbs home, treat them just like flowers. Leave them bound, trim steams, and place them in a glass of water and keep in the fridge.

SPRIGHTLY SALAD OF WATERCRESS & PECAN CHÈVRE MEDALLIONS

16 oz. goat cheese (chèvre)

1 c roasted pecans, roughly chopped

2 T white wine vinegar

1 T whole-grain mustard

2 T minced shallots

1 t minced fresh parsley

½ t minced fresh thyme

6 T olive oil

Salt and pepper

2 bunches watercress, trimmed, cleaned, spun or blotted dry

3 oz arugula, cleaned, spun or blotted dry

Preheat oven to 200°F. Line a sheet pan with parchment paper.

Cut cheese into 8 medallions. Press into pecans to coat. Place on prepared sheet pan and bake 2 minutes to heat through.

For vinaigrette, whisk together vinegar, mustard, shallots, parsley, and thyme. Gradually whisk in oil. Season to taste with salt and pepper.

In a large bowl, toss together watercress, arugula, and vinaigrette.

Serve topped with warm pecan chèvre medallions.

Makes 8 servings

WARM ROASTED SWEET POTATO MAPLE BACON SALAD

3 c sweet potatoes, skin on, cut into bite size pieces

Olive oil

Salt and pepper

½ lb thick bacon, snipped into 1-inch pieces

1 c real maple syrup

3 T rice vinegar

2 T fresh rosemary, chopped

6 c salad greens, cut, rinsed and spun dry

½ c roasted pumpkin seeds

Preheat oven to 400°F. In a large bowl, toss the potatoes, olive oil, salt, and pepper. Spread onto a sheet pan. Roast approximately 30 minutes or until fork tender.

In a large skillet, cook bacon until crisp.

Meanwhile, combine maple syrup, vinegar, and rosemary in a small bowl.

When bacon is crisp, remove from skillet and drain on paper towels. Add 3 tablespoons of the bacon grease to dressing mixture. Whisk to combine and season to taste with salt and pepper.

In a large bowl, toss greens with sparse dressing, adding more as needed – careful not to douse.

Mound on a serving platter and top with sweet potato, bacon, and pumpkin seeds.

PROSCUITTO & NECTARINE SALAD

2 T olive oil

2 T white balsamic vinegar

2 T Dijon mustard

2 T honey

1 shallot, minced

8 mint leaves, chopped

Salt and pepper

8 oz prosciutto, snipped with scissors

3 c arugula, rinsed and spun dry

2 c curly endive, cut, rinsed and spun dry

4 nectarines, pitted and thinly sliced

½ c toasted almonds

Whisk together olive oil, vinegar, mustard, honey, shallot, and mint leaves. Season to taste with salt and pepper. Refrigerate until ready to serve.

In a small skillet, heat 1 tablespoon oil over medium heat. Add prosciutto and cook until nicely brown and crisp.

In a bowl, toss together arugula, endive, nectarines, and almonds. Toss salad with minimal dressing, adding more as needed.

Mound on platter and garnish with warm prosciutto.

Makes 4 to 6 servings

FESTIVE QUINOA SALAD

2 c chicken broth or stock

1 c quinoa

⅓ c apple cider vinegar

⅓ c olive oil

1 medium orange, zested and juiced

2 T pure maple syrup

1 c slivered almonds, toasted

½ c diced celery

½ c dried cranberries

½ c flat-leaf Italian parsley, coarsely chopped

¼ c fresh mint, coarsely chopped

2 green onions, thinly sliced

Salt and pepper

To extend the volume and make into a fluffier salad, toss this recipe with nice peppery arugula.

In a medium saucepan combine broth and quinoa. Bring to a boil. Reduce heat to low. Simmer, covered, 15 minutes or until quinoa is cooked through but still al dente.

In a small bowl, whisk together next apple cider vinegar, olive oil, orange, and maple syrup. Add almonds, celery, cranberries, parsley, mint, and green onions. Toss to combine. Season to taste with salt and pepper.

Serve warm or at room temperature.

Makes 4 to 6 servings

CRISPY COD MARKET SALAD

3 egg whites

¼ c cornstarch

1 c panko crumbs

1 t each salt and pepper

1 t granulated garlic

6 to 8 cod loins, rinsed and blotted dry with paper towels

2 t butter

2 t canola oil

Cilantro leaves

Black sesame seeds

1 recipe Chili Garlic Sauce (page 143)

SALAD

2 c baby bok choy, thinly sliced

2 c Savoy cabbage, thinly sliced

2 carrots, julienned

1 medium red bell pepper, julienned

1 c mung bean sprouts

1 small jicama, julienned

4 to 6 scallions, green parts only, cut diagonally

In a serving bowl, toss together all salad ingredients. Set aside.

In a shallow dish, whisk together egg whites and cornstarch. In second shallow dish, combine panko, salt, pepper, and garlic. Dip each cod loin first in egg white mixture, then in crumb mixture to coat.

In a large skillet, heat butter and oil over medium high heat. Sear cod, in batches, 1½ minutes on all sides until golden and crisp. Don't overcrowd skillet or cod will steam rather than sear.

Top salad with cod loins. Drizzle with Chili Garlic Sauce. Garnish with cilantro and sesame seeds.

Makes 6 servings

FALL APPLE & WALNUT SALAD WITH MAPLE BALSAMIC VINAIGRETTE

⅓ c balsamic vinegar

¼ c canola oil

1 small shallot, diced

1 T pure maple syrup

Salt and pepper

6 c freshly cut, washed, spun and drained greens (your favorite lettuce)

1 red or green apple, skin on, cored and sliced thin

½ c chopped dates

½ c crumbled feta cheese

½ c walnuts, toasted and coarsely chopped

For vinaigrette, in a small bowl combine vinegar, oil, shallot, and maple syrup. Season to taste with salt and pepper.

In a large bowl, toss together the salad greens, apple, dates, feta, and walnuts. Add the vinaigrette a small amount at a time and toss to coat, adding additional as needed.

Serve mounded on a platter.

Makes 4 to 6 servings

ZESTY LIME, PINEAPPLE & AVOCADO WITH BABY GREENS

Zest of 1 lime

Juice of 2 limes

2 T white balsamic vinegar

1 T olive oil

¼ t kosher salt

Black pepper

5 oz baby greens, washed and spun dry

1 medium hass avocado, diced

¾ c diced fresh pineapple

¼ c scallion, green parts only, thinly sliced

¼ c toasted almonds, walnuts or pecans

For dressing, in a screw-top jar combine lime zest, juice, vinegar, oil, salt, and pepper.

In a large bowl, combine remaining ingredients. Add dressing and toss to combine.

Mound on a pretty platter to serve.

I can do all things through Christ, because he gives me strength.

PHILIPPIANS 4:13

(I live by this.)

2 - Into the chest their hands they pushed
And laid upon the coral beach
An Emerald and a Ruby.
     Sandra Cooper & Judy Johnson.

3 - Into the chest they delved again
These two excited men.
And drew forth jewels worth a king's ransom
In the form of a dangling tiara,
     Girls group.

4 - Next from the chest they withdrew
a necklace that sparkled like the dew.
     Girls Trio.

5 - A pair of Charm bracelets were next in line
A Charming duet I'm sure you'll find.
     Piano duet.

6 - A pin set with diamonds and gold
Was next for their eyes to behold.
     Judy - Top

7 - Among the gold coins they found
a plain wedding band
That some fair lady had worn upon her
snow white hand

soups

54   BACON LENTIL SOUP

55   CREMINI MUSHROOM SHERRY BISQUE

56   ITALIAN "LOVE APPLE" SOUP WITH SPINACH PESTO

57   ROASTED APPLE & BUTTERNUT SQUASH BISQUE

58   CREAMY CORN & BACON CHOWDER

59   WILD RICE SOUP WITH SMOKED SAUSAGE

60   SOUL SOOTHING LOADED BAKED POTATO SOUP

61   ROASTED RED PEPPER BISQUE WITH CROUTON HEARTS

62   WHITE GAZPACHO

63   SASSY CHARRED CORN CHOWDER

BACON LENTIL SOUP

2 T olive oil

½ c onion, chopped

½ c celery, chopped

½ c carrot, chopped

2 cloves garlic, thinly sliced

7 c chicken broth

2 c dried lentils, your choice of color

½ t thyme, dried

1 bay leaf

Salt and pepper

4 slices thick bacon, fried, crumbled

Scallion, thinly slived

Fresh parsley, chopped

In a Dutch oven, heat oil over medium high heat. Add onion, celery, carrot, and garlic. Cook, stirring, until onion is translucent.

Add broth, lentils, thyme, and bay leaf. Bring to boil then simmer for 40 minutes or until lentils are tender. (Check lentil package for cook time recommendation as it varies depending on color.) Remove bay leaf. Season to taste with salt and pepper.

Serve in bowls and garnish with crumbled bacon, scallion, and parsley.

Makes 8 to 10 servings

CREMINI MUSHROOM SHERRY BISQUE

8 T (1 stick) butter, room temperature

2 c onion, diced

1¾ c celery, diced

3 garlic cloves, minced

9 c (1 lb) fresh cremini mushrooms, sliced

½ c dry white wine

½ c dry sherry

¼ c all-purpose flour

8 c chicken or vegetable stock

½ c heavy cream

Salt and pepper

In a large pot, melt 6 tablespoons of the butter over medium high heat. Add onion, celery, and garlic and cook about 8 minutes or until onion is translucent. Add mushrooms and cook about 4 minutes until they begin to soften. Add white wine and sherry. Bring to a boil. Cook 6 minutes or until liquid is reduced to a glaze.

In small bowl, mix remaining 2 tablespoons of butter and flour until they form a smooth paste. Add flour paste to mushroom mixture in pot, stirring until mixture melts and coats vegetables.

Gradually mix in stock. Bring to boil, stirring frequently. Reduce heat to medium low and simmer about 10 minutes until mushrooms are tender. Stir often.

Stir in cream and heat through. Season to taste with salt and pepper.

Using an immersion blender, blend to desired texture. Or, let cool slightly, and purée in a blender or food processor in batches.

Makes approximately one gallon

TERRIE'S TIDBIT

One thing I stress is that God forbid there be any leftover wine. There's never a reason to throw it away. Use it as an ingredient in a stew, soup, or sauce. The worst thing that could happen is that it will turn into vinegar.

ITALIAN "LOVE APPLE" SOUP WITH SPINACH PESTO

2 T olive oil

1½ c red onion, chopped

¼ t crushed red pepper

3 cloves garlic, minced

Three 14.5-oz cans diced tomatoes

1¾ cup water

2 sprigs thyme

2 t vegetable base (Better Than Bouillon®)

Salt and pepper

Sugar (if you would like it less bitter)

1 recipe Spinach Pesto (page 133)

A tomato in Italian culture is called a "love apple." I created this recipe for a private Valentine's Day cooking class.

In a medium or large saucepan, heat oil over medium high. Add onion, crushed red pepper, and garlic. Cook, stirring, 4 to 5 minutes.

Add tomatoes, water, thyme, and vegetable base. Bring to a boil. Season to taste with salt, pepper, and sugar. Hold on low heat while making pesto (if not made ahead of time).

Serve soup in bowls and drizzle pesto around the top – pretty and tasty!

Makes 6 to 8 servings

ROASTED APPLE & BUTTERNUT SQUASH BISQUE

2 lbs butternut squash, peeled and cubed

3 medium shallots, peeled and chunked

2 medium cloves garlic, whole or halved depending on size

2 T olive oil

2 Granny Smith apples, peeled, cored and cut in chunks

¾ c water

¼ c dry sherry

2 T vegetable base, (Better Than Bouillon®)

One 12-oz can evaporated milk

Salt and pepper

Fresh grated nutmeg

Preheat oven to 350°F. Toss together squash, shallots, garlic, and olive oil in a large bowl. Spread evenly on sheet pan and roast 20 minutes.

Add apples to the pan and bake another 20 minutes until baked through, fork tender.

Meanwhile, in a Dutch oven over medium high heat bring water, sherry, and vegetable base to a boil.

Add roasted squash and apples to Dutch oven and return to a boil. Add milk and heat through. Do not boil or it will curdle.

Purée using an immersion blender. Or, let cool slightly, and purée in a blender or food processor in batches. Season to taste with salt, pepper, and nutmeg.

Makes 6 to 8 servings

CREAMY CORN & BACON CHOWDER

1 T canola oil

2 c frozen corn, thawed

4 strips bacon, diced

1 c red onion, diced

1 c red bell pepper, diced

2 t garlic, minced

6 c chicken stock

2 c red or Yukon gold potato, skin on, diced

One 14.75-oz can creamed corn

2 t Worcestershire sauce

Salt and pepper

2 T butter, softened

2 T all-purpose flour

6 T cream

Fresh parsley, coarsely chopped

In large saucepot, heat oil on medium high heat. Add corn, bacon, onion, bell pepper, and garlic. Cook 3 minutes or until vegetables are tender. Add chicken stock, potato, creamed corn, and Worcestershire sauce. Bring to a boil. Cover and simmer 20 minutes. Season to taste with salt and pepper.

In a medium bowl, combine butter and flour. Mix 1 c of soup into butter mixture, then add back into soup and stir to combine.

Simmer 5 minutes until thickened and bubbly. Stir in cream to enrichen.

Garnish with sprinkling of parsley.

Makes 8 to 10 servings

WILD RICE SOUP WITH SMOKED SAUSAGE

6 oz kielbasa sausage, cut in half moons

6 c chicken broth

½ c wild rice

2 c corn

1 large carrot, diced

1 red onion, julienned

2 to 4 cloves garlic, minced

2 T cold water

2 T cornstarch

Salt and pepper

¼ c fresh parsley, coarsely chopped

In a large pot, cook sausage over medium high heat until browned. Remove from pot.

Add broth to pot and bring to a boil. Add rice. Reduce heat, cover, and simmer 45 minutes or until tender and starting to split.

Add carrot, onion, garlic, and sausage to pot. Return to a boil. Reduce heat and simmer, covered, 10 minutes or until tender.

In a small bowl, whisk together water and cornstarch. Slowly add to pot while whisking continuously. Cook and stir until thickened and bubbly. Season to taste with salt and pepper. Add parsley right before serving.

Makes 6 to 8 servings

SOUL SOOTHING LOADED BAKED POTATO SOUP

5 medium russet potatoes

½ c butter

2 to 3 stalks celery, diced

½ red onion diced

1 T chicken base (Better Than Bouillon®)

½ c all-purpose flour

6 c milk

1 c sour cream

Salt and white pepper

Cheddar cheese, shredded

Fresh green onion or chives, chopped

Bacon, crisp-cooked

Butter (optional)

Baking potatoes adds a roasted flavor. Boiling potatoes causes some of the flavor to escape.

Preheat oven to 400°F.

Pierce potatoes several times with a fork. Place on baking sheet or directly on oven grates. Bake until tender, 65 to 75 minutes depending upon size. Let cool partially and chop.

In a large pot, melt butter over medium heat. Add baked potatoes, celery, onion, and chicken base. Cook and stir 5 minutes or until vegetables are tender. Add flour. Stir until smooth. Cook 3 to 4 minutes to cook out any floury taste. Slowly pour in milk and stir until thickened and bubbly. Whisk in cream. Season to taste with salt and pepper.

Garnish each serving with cheese, green onion or chives, bacon, and butter (for indulgence).

Makes 6 to 8 servings

ROASTED RED PEPPER BISQUE WITH CROUTON HEARTS

6 medium carrots, skin on, cut into chunks

4 medium red bell peppers, cut into chunks

2 stalks celery, cut into small chunks

1 large onion, cut into chunks

Olive oil

Salt and pepper

4 c chicken stock

4 c heavy cream

One 6-oz can tomato paste

8 fresh basil leaves, coarsely chopped

2 T garlic, minced

Milk (optional)

Bread slice(s)

Nonstick cooking spray

Herbs

Another recipe created for Valentine's Day, thus the red color and heart-shaped croutons.

Preheat oven to 375°F.

In a large bowl, toss carrots, peppers, celery, and onion with olive oil, salt, and pepper. Spread onto two sheet pans. Roast 40 minutes or until tender, stirring after 10 minutes.

In a Dutch oven combine chicken stock, cream, tomato paste, basil, and garlic. Add roasted vegetables and bring to a boil. Blend until smooth with an immersion blender, or cool slightly and purée in batches in a blender or food processor.

Preheat broiler.

Using a heart shaped cookie cutter, cut out hearts from bread slice (or cut into 1-inch cubes). Place on a baking sheet. Coat with nonstick spray and sprinkle with herbs of choice.

Broil 4 to 5 inches from the heat just long enough to toast – watch closely! Flip over and toast back side, too.

Serve soup in bowls. Top with crouton heart.

Makes 8 to 10 servings

WHITE GAZPACHO

1 large Hothouse cucumber, peeled, seeded, and chopped

2¼ c seedless green grapes (save some for garnish)

1½ c blanched, slivered almonds (save some for garnish)

1½ c vegetable broth, chilled

2 T fresh dill, chopped (save some for garnish)

½ small shallot

1 small clove garlic

¼ c olive oil

2 T dry Sherry

1 T sherry vinegar

Salt and white pepper

This summer soup is eaten cold and can be served in a bowl or in a cup for sipping. The dill makes it so refreshing!

In a food processor, combine cucumbers, grapes, almonds, broth, drill, shallot, and garlic. Pulse to purée.

With motor running, gradually drizzle in olive oil, checking for taste. Less is better. Process until very smooth. Add sherry and vinegar and purée for 1 minute. The finished texture should be smooth, creamy, and just a bit grainy from the almonds.

Season to taste with salt and pepper, then transfer to a bowl. Cover and refrigerate until well chilled.

When ready to serve, thinly slice remaining grapes and finely chop remaining almonds. Pour gazpacho into bowls, and garnish with grapes, almonds, and remaining dill.

Makes 4 to 6 servings

TERRIE'S TIDBIT

I don't want people to think they have to have a fresh bottle of wine for cooking. I buy boxed wine for cooking.

SASSY CHARRED CORN CHOWDER

2 c corn off the cob, charred

4 slices of slab bacon, diced

1 c diced red onion

½ c diced celery

½ c diced carrot

2 c milk

2 c heavy cream

2 t chicken base (Better Than Bouillon®)

2 T cornstarch

2 T cold water

Fresh chives, parsley or scallions, chopped

In a large skillet, cook bacon over medium heat until crisp. Remove bacon from skillet and drain on paper towels.

Add onion, celery, carrot, and charred corn to bacon drippings in skillet. Cook over medium heat 5 minutes or until tender.

In a medium saucepan combine milk, cream, and chicken base. Bring to a boil over medium heat.

In a small bowl, whisk together cornstarch and water. Gradually add to cream mixture, stirring continuously so as not to clump. Cook until thickened and bubbly. Add vegetable mixture and heat through.

Serve into bowls and garnish with crumbled bacon and chives, parsley or scallions.

Makes 6 to 8 servings

       Among the gold coins they found

       A plain wedding band

       That some fair lady had worn

       Upon her lily white hand.

~~IX~~
X   Sandra Cooper

       "Our treasures we have shown

       Now we must be on our way.

But If you ~~will~~ look out, o'er the bay of Capri

       At the close of most any day

Pirates *Our* ship with Red Sails In The Sunset

       ~~We are sure you will see."~~ *"be able to see"*

          Pirates pick up chest and leave stage.

XI   Accordion--- Kathy Adams

       To entertain you to-night

       Has been our delight

       And we hope you enjoyed being here

       If you did, and we trust that you did

       Wont you please come again next year?

                   The End

The third of the three pages (from page 52).

sides

66 BAKED RICE PILAF

67 BRAISED BRUSSELS SPROUTS WITH BACON

68 CREAMY POLENTA WITH ROASTED CORN & SWEET RED PEPPERS

69 EGGPLANT PARMESAN

70 LOBSTER MAC & CHEESE

71 ROASTED BUTTERNUT SQUASH & SAGE GNOCCHI

72 GARLIC SMASHED POTATOES

73 HEARTY BLACK BEAN GUMBO

74 SPAGHETTI SQUASH WITH SPINACH PESTO & TOMATO

75 GRILLED ROMAINE HEARTS WITH TANGY SHERRY DRESSING

76 SUMMERTIME SUCCOTASH

77 MARKET BAKERY BREAD

BAKED RICE PILAF

2 T butter

2 small or 1 medium to large leek, cut lengthwise, rinse through, then slice crosswise into half moons

1 c celery, sliced

3 cloves garlic, sliced

1½ c basmati rice

3 c hot chicken stock

1 c shredded Parmesan

1 c frozen peas, thawed

½ c pine nuts, toasted

¼ c parsley, chopped

1 T lemon zest

1½ t each salt and pepper

I love to do rice pilaf with my cooking classes. It's super simple and makes a nice side dish.

Preheat oven to 350°F.

In large saucepan, heat butter medium high. Cook leek, celery, and garlic briefly until softened. Add rice and stir to coat, 2 to 3 minutes.

Add stock and stir. Cover pan and place in oven for 25 to 30 minutes or until tender.

Mix in Parmesan, peas, nuts, parsley, lemon zest, salt, and pepper.

Makes 4 to 6 servings

BRAISED BRUSSELS SPROUTS WITH BACON

1 T olive oil

4 slices thick-cut peppered bacon, cut crosswise in 1-inch pieces

1 medium red onion, julienned

2 to 3 cloves garlic, thinly sliced

2 lbs Brussels sprouts, washed and halved

2 c chicken stock

2 T cornstarch

2 T cold water

Salt and pepper

In a large skillet, heat oil over medium high heat. Add bacon. Cook until halfway done, 5 minutes. Add onion and garlic. Continue cooking until bacon is crisp and onion is tender, another 5 minutes. Remove mixture from skillet and drain on a paper towel.

Add Brussels sprouts to skillet and cook about 5 minutes or until slightly softened. Add stock, bring to boil, and cover. Turn heat down to simmer and cook another 5 minutes or until tender. They should remain bright green.

In a small bowl, whisk together cornstarch and water. Add cornstarch mixture, stirring continuously so as not to clump.

Season to taste with salt and pepper and garnish with reserved bacon mixture.

Makes 4 to 6 servings

CREAMY POLENTA WITH ROASTED CORN & SWEET RED PEPPERS

¾ c frozen corn, thawed

¾ c red bell pepper, diced

⅓ c shallots, chopped

Olive oil

Salt and pepper

5 c chicken stock

1 T fresh thyme or sub 1 t dried thyme

1 T garlic, minced

1 c instant polenta cornmeal

½ c Parmesan cheese, shredded

Preheat oven to 350°F. Line a sheet pan with parchment paper.

In a medium bowl, toss together corn, red pepper, and shallots. Drizzle with olive oil and sprinkle with salt and pepper. Pour out onto the pan. Roast 30 minutes, or until tender, stirring halway through.

In a large saucepan, bring stock, thyme, and garlic to a boil. Gradually whisk in polenta in a steady stream. Reduce heat to medium, cook about 10 to 15 minutes, whisking until thick and creamy. Stir in roasted vegetables and cheese. Heat through.

Season to taste with salt and pepper. Transfer to bowl to serve. Option to save some of the vegetables to use for garnish.

Makes 6 to 8 servings

EGGPLANT PARMESAN

1 c all-purpose flour

1 t each salt and pepper

3 eggs

1 c wheat germ

⅔ c panko crumbs

½ c Parmesan cheese, grated

2 medium eggplant, cut into ½ to 1-inch slices

2 T olive oil

6 cloves garlic, minced

1½ t crushed red pepper

Four 14.5-oz cans diced tomatoes

2 c olives, coarsely chopped (Your choice Greek, black, green. I like green.)

⅓ c fresh basil, julienned

3 T capers

1 t fresh thyme

¾ c Italian flat leaf parsley, coarsely chopped

1 lb fresh mozzarella cheese, thinly sliced

Preheat oven to 400°F. Line a baking sheet with parchment paper and top with a cooling rack.

In a shallow dish, combine flour, salt, and pepper. In another shallow dish, lightly beat eggs. In a third shallow dish, combine wheat germ, panko and Parmesan.

Dip eggplant slices first in flour mixture, then in egg, then in crumb mixture to coat. Place on prepared baking sheet. Bake 15 minutes or until browned and tender. Reserve any remaining crumb mixture.

Reduce oven temperature to 375°F.

In a large saucepan, heat oil over medium high heat. Add garlic and crushed red pepper. Cook and stir 1 minute or until fragrant. Add tomatoes, olives, basil, capers, and thyme. Bring to a boil. Reduce heat and simmer. Stir in parsley. Season to taste with salt and pepper. You won't need much salt, but will need pepper for sure.

In 9x13 baking dish, arrange ingredients in this order: one-fourth of the sauce, half of the eggplant, one-fourth of the sauce, half of the cheese, the remaining eggplant, one-fourth of the sauce, remaining cheese, remaining sauce, and any remaining crumb mixture.

Bake uncovered for 30 minutes or until hot and bubbly.

Makes 10 to 12 servings

sides

LOBSTER MAC & CHEESE

Two 8-oz lobster tails

1 lb favorite pasta

2 c milk

1 shallot, diced

2 cloves garlic, thinly sliced

2 lbs smoked Gouda, cheddar, Parmesan and/or Asiago cheeses, shredded

Salt and pepper

½ c Parmesan cheese, grated (for garnish)

½ panko crumbs

1 T dried parsley flakes

2 t paprika

Preheat oven to 350°F. Butter 6 to 8 ramekins or au gratin dishes.

Cook pasta according to package directions. Reserve 1 cup of pasta water from draining.

In large pot, bring reserved pasta water, milk, shallot, garlic, and lobster shells to a simmer. Reduce heat and simmer 15 minutes. Remove and discard shells. Chop the lobster meat.

Stir in cheese gradually so as not to clump. Season to taste with salt and white pepper. Stir in pasta and lobster.

Pour into ramekins or au gratin dishes.

In a small bowl, combine ½ cup Parmesan, panko, parsley, and paprika. Sprinkle over tops and bake 30 minutes or until bubbly and tops are golden brown.

Makes 6 to 8 servings

ROASTED BUTTERNUT SQUASH & SAGE GNOCCHI

1 lb butternut squash, peeled, seeds and fibrous material removed, cut in 1-inch chunks

3 T olive oil

2 t salt

¼ t white pepper

1 t dry parsley

1¼ c all-purpose flour (plus more for coating)

½ cup (1 stick) butter

8 oz portabella mushrooms, cut into medium slices

¼ c fresh sage, cut in thin strips

Cheese of choice, smoked Gouda or Gruyère, shredded

Preheat oven to 350°F

In a large bowl, toss together squash, 1 tablespoon olive oil, 1½ teaspoons salt, and white pepper. Pour out onto a sheet pan. Bake 20 to 25 minutes or until fork tender with some brown.

Place squash back in the bowl and mash with a potato masher until smooth. Add 2 tablespoons olive oil, ½ teaspoon salt, and parsley. Mash again to combine. Add flour and work until smooth (not tacky) with your hands. Divide into fourths and roll each into ½-inch ropes. Cover with a damp kitchen towel and allow to rest 15 to 20 minutes.

Cut into ½-inch pieces on the diagonal. Toss in additional flour to coat edges. Place gently into deep pot of salted boiling water, in batches. Gnocchi will float when done, about 3 minutes. Drain.

In a large skillet, melt butter on medium high heat and allow to brown. Add mushrooms and cook until tender, or liquid exudes. Add gnocchi and sage and heat through.

Serve with cheese.

Makes 4 to 6 servings

GARLIC SMASHED POTATOES

1½ lb baby red potatoes, scrubbed and cut into chunks

¾ c sour cream

½ c (1 stick) butter

2 t fresh garlic, minced

1½ t each salt and pepper

2 T fresh chives, minced

Splash milk or cream

Place potatoes in a pot and add enough cold water to cover. Bring to a boil. Reduce heat and simmer 30 minutes or until tender. Drain and place in mixing bowl.

Combine sour cream, butter, garlic, salt, and pepper and cook for 10 minutes over medium heat.

Add hot butter mixture and chives to the potatoes.

Mix to desired consistency, adding milk, if necessary.

Makes 4 to 6 servings

HEARTY BLACK BEAN GUMBO

2 T olive oil

2 medium onions, chopped

3 to 4 medium carrots, sliced

2 medium green bell peppers, seeded and chopped

2 medium red bell peppers, seeded and chopped

4 T chili powder, or to taste

1 t gumbo filé powder (optional), a regional thickener found in most spice sections

3 c chicken or vegetable stock

Two 15-oz cans black beans, do not drain

2 c frozen okra

Salt and freshly ground pepper to taste

Serve over white rice to make this dish an entrée.

Heat the olive oil in a large skillet over medium heat and cook the onion, carrot, and peppers covered for 5 minutes or until tender. Add the chili and filé powder and cook 3 more minutes. Add the stock, beans, okra, salt, and pepper and bring to a boil. Reduce the heat and simmer uncovered for 10 minutes, or until okra is fork tender but not mushy.

Makes 6 to 8 servings

sides

SPAGHETTI SQUASH WITH SPINACH PESTO & TOMATO

1 spaghetti squash (about 4 pounds), halved lengthwise, seeds removed

Olive oil

Salt and pepper

1 to 2 tomatoes, diced and drained

½ cup pine nuts, toasted

Hard cheese, shredded

1 recipe Spinach Pesto (page 133)

Preheat oven to 400°F.

Brush cut sides of squash with oil and sprinkle with salt and pepper to taste. Place squash, cut sides up, on a rimmed baking pan. Roast 30 to 40 minutes. Roast less time for a crunchy texture, or more time for more tender texture. If it roasts for too long, there will be no definition.

Let cool slightly, until able to handle. Scrape squash with a fork to remove flesh in long strands.

In a serving bowl, mix together spaghetti squash and spinach pesto. Add tomatoes and ½ cup pine nuts. Top with fresh shredded hard cheese.

Makes 4 to 6 servings

GRILLED ROMAINE HEARTS WITH TANGY SHERRY DRESSING

¼ c canola oil

1 T sherry vinegar

1 T dry sherry

1 t Dijon mustard

1 t minced garlic

Pinch sugar

Salt and pepper

2 to 4 hearts of romaine lettuce, if large can be cut into thirds

Nonstick olive oil cooking spray

Manchego cheese, shredded

Preheat an outdoor grill to medium high heat.

In a small bowl, whisk together oil, sherry vinegar, dry sherry, Dijon, garlic, and sugar. Season to taste with salt and pepper. Chill in the refrigerator.

Trim tops of lettuce if discolored and cut in half lengthwise. Spray cut sides of lettuce with nonstick spray.

Place lettuce on a grill rack, cut side down. Grill 2 minutes or until slightly charred. Give a quarter turn and grill 1 to 2 minutes more to char to your liking.

Remove from grill and sprinkle with shredded cheese immediately to melt. Serve topped with dressing.

Makes 8 to 10 servings

SUMMERTIME SUCCOTASH

3 T butter

1 c of vegetables per person, mix of below or your choice

Edamame

Corn cut from cob

Peas

Broccoli florets

Various colors of bell pepper, chopped

Onion, chopped

Cauliflower florets

Canned lima beans, drained

Tomato, chopped

Salt and pepper

Fresh thyme, chopped

Great on the side of grilled pork chops. Now that says summertime!

In a large shallow skillet, sauté vegetables over medium hear in order of firmness, e.g. onion, edamame, broccoli, cauliflower. Add beans and tomato just to heat through. Season to taste with salt, pepper, and thyme.

MARKET BAKERY BREAD

1 c warm water

2 T sugar

2¼ t (1 pkg) rapid rising dry yeast

3½ to 4 c flour

1 T minced garlic

2 t Italian seasoning

¼ c olive oil

2 T water

1 T Kosher salt

Nonstick cooking spray

Cornmeal for dusting

Olive oil

Sea salt

Dried parsley

I make homemade bread for every cooking class. It is a much sought-after recipe. You can have homemade bread in less than two hours!

In bowl of a mixer, combine warm water, sugar, and yeast, stirring to dissolve. Let stand 3 minutes until foam appears. Add flour, garlic, and Italian seasoning.

In a small bowl, combine oil, 2 tablespoons of water, and salt, stirring to dissolve. Add to mixing bowl.

Using a dough hook, start mixing on low speed. When dough starts to come together, increase speed to medium.

Form dough into ball and place into an oiled bowl, turning to coat. Cover with plastic wrap and let rise in a warm space about 1 hour or until dough ball doubles in size.

Preheat oven to 425°F. Line a sheetpan with parchment paper. Coat paper with nonstick spray and sprinkle with cornmeal.

Divide dough in half and shape into 2 round or oblong loaves. Lay loaves on prepared sheetpan. Cover with plastic wrap and let rest 15 minutes.

Remove plastic and bake on a bottom oven rack for 15 to 20 minutes, rotating after 10 minutes for even baking.

Once out of the oven, brush with olive oil and a fine sprinkle of sea salt and parsley.

Makes 2 loaves

"Bringing friends and family back around the table" is one of my mantras, so there is no more perfect food for the cover of my book than paella. The traditional way to serve this traditional rice-based Spanish dish is to place the pan in the middle of the table, with everyone serving themselves from the dish. It's a very social meal... from a very social chef.

pastas & rice dishes

- 80 *ON THE COVER* CHICKEN & SHRIMP PAELLA
- 81 SPANISH SAFFRON CHORIZO PAELLA
- 82 CREMINI & LEEK RISOTTO WITH BLUEBERRIES
- 83 GREEK SHRIMP PASTA
- 84 TOMATO VODKA CHICKEN SPAGHETTI
- 85 SEARED SCALLOPS ATOP SQUASH & APRICOT RISOTTO
- 86 CHIANTI BOLOGNESE ALLA PAPPARDELLE
- 87 IOWA CHARRED CORN & JALAPEÑO RISOTTO
- 88 AUTUMN PASTA WITH BUTTERNUT SQUASH PROSCIUTTO SAUCE
- 89 STUFFED PASTA SHELLS
- 90 LEEK, FENNEL & APRICOT RISOTTO
- 91 ITALIAN SAUSAGE & ARUGULA PASTA
- 92 THAI "DRUNKEN NOODLES" WITH PLUMP SHRIMP
- 93 ORZO PASTA WITH BACON, OLIVES & FETA
- 94 BUTTERNUT SQUASH & ROOT VEGETABLE LASAGNA
- 95 STRAWBERRY RISOTTO WITH BASIL CHIFFONADE

ON THE COVER
CHICKEN & SHRIMP PAELLA

6 T olive oil

1 c onions, minced

1 small red bell pepper, seeded and julienned

1 small green bell pepper, seeded and julienned

1 c canned diced tomatoes, drained

1 T garlic, minced

1 T fresh thyme, minced

1 t each salt and pepper

3 c long grain rice

¼ t ground saffron or saffron threads

½ c dry white wine

5 to 6 c chicken stock, heated to a simmer

2 lbs skinless boneless chicken breast halves, cut in 1-inch cubes

8 oz cooked chorizo, cut thin on diagonal

2 lbs medium shrimp, peeled and deveined

One 14-oz can quartered artichoke hearts, drained

1 c frozen peas

Lemon wedges

Flat leaf parsley, minced

Paella is a Spanish dish of saffron-flavored rice combined with a variety of meats, shellfish, and vegetables. It's named after the special two-handled pan in which it's prepared and served. The pan is wide, shallow and 13 to 14 inches in diameter.

Preheat oven to 400°F.

In a paella pan (or large skillet) heat 2 tablespoons olive oil over medium high heat. Add onion and peppers and cook 2 minutes or until softened. Add tomatoes, garlic, thyme, salt, and pepper. Stir until most of liquid has evaporated. Stir in rice and saffron to coat. Add wine and stir until evaporated. Pour in 3 cups of the chicken stock and bring to boil over high heat.

Remove from heat and arrange chicken and chorizo on top of rice.

Set on lowest rack of the oven. Bake uncovered for 20 minutes. **Do not stir paella after it has been in the oven.**

Scatter shrimp, peas, and artichokes on top of the mixture and bake 5 to 10 minutes more or until liquid has been absorbed and rice is tender. If necessary add remaining stock – may not use it all.

Remove from oven and let stand 5 minutes at room temperature before serving.

Serve garnished with lemon and minced flat leaf parsley.

This will make two full paella pans. Halve the recipe for one pan.

SPANISH SAFFRON CHORIZO PAELLA

3 T olive oil

½ c onions, diced

1 small red bell pepper, seeded and julienned

One 14.5-oz. can diced tomatoes

1 T garlic, thinly sliced

1 t dry thyme

½ t each salt and pepper

1¼ c long grain rice

½ c dry white wine

¼ t ground saffron or saffron threads

1½ lb chorizo

2½ to 3 c simmering chicken stock

½ c frozen peas

½ c canned/jarred artichoke hearts, quartered, drained

Lemon wedges

Flat leaf parsley, minced

Chorizo is a highly seasoned, coarsely ground pork sausage flavored with garlic, chili powder and other spices. It's widely used in both Mexican and Spanish cooking. Mexican chorizo is made with fresh pork, while the Spanish version uses smoked pork. The casing should be removed before cooking. Chorizo makes a tasty addition to many dishes including casseroles, soups, stew and enchiladas.

Preheat oven to 400°F.

In paella pan (or large skillet) heat oil over medium high until hot. Add onion and pepper and cook, stirring for 5 minutes or until softened. Add tomatoes, garlic, thyme, salt, and pepper. Cook stirring 5 minutes more or until most of liquid has evaporated and mixture is thick. Add rice and stir to coat. Add wine and saffron. Pour in 2¼ c stock and bring to a boil over high heat.

Remove from heat and arrange chorizo on top of rice. Set on bottom oven rack and bake uncovered for 20 minutes.

Scatter peas and artichokes on top and bake 5 to 10 minutes more until liquid has been absorbed and the rice is tender. If necessary add remaining ¾ cup of stock. **Do not stir paella after it has been in the oven.**

Let stand 5 minutes at room temperature before serving.

Serve garnished with lemon and parsley.

Makes one paella pan, approximately 6 to 8 servings

pastas & rice dishes

CREMINI & LEEK RISOTTO WITH BLUEBERRIES

6 T butter

1 c sliced cremini mushrooms

2 leeks, pale green and white parts, halved lengthwise and cut crosswise into half moons

½ c dried blueberries

1 t garlic

1 c Arborio rice

½ c dry white wine, heated

3 c chicken stock, heated

¼ c fresh parsley, chopped

Salt and pepper

Fresh Parmesan, Asiago, or Manchego cheese, grated

In a large saucepan, heat 2 tablespoons of butter over medium high heat. Add mushrooms, leeks, blueberries, and garlic. Cook for 5 minutes until tender. Remove from pan and set aside.

Cook remaining 4 tablespoons of butter in the pan until melted. Add rice and cook 3 minutes, stirring to coat rice with butter. Add wine and stir constantly until absorbed. Ladle in stock until it is all incorporated or just until rice is at desired consistency.

Rice should be tender, not too soft or chalky. May need additional hot water to accomplish this texture.

Add reserved vegetable mixture. Stir in parsley and salt and pepper to taste.

Serve topped with grated cheese.

Makes 4 to 6 servings

GREEK SHRIMP PASTA

4 T olive oil

1 lb E-Z peel raw shrimp, peeled, tail on or off – your preference

4 cloves garlic, thinly sliced

½ t crushed red pepper

½ c dry white wine

Two 14.5 oz cans diced tomatoes, undrained

6 scallions, thinly sliced diagonally

2 t dry oregano

1½ t lemon zest

Salt and pepper

1 lb favorite pasta, cooked according to package directions

6 oz arugula, rinsed and spun or blotted dry

Two 4-oz packages crumbled basil tomato feta cheese

½ c pine nuts, toasted

In a medium or large skillet, heat oil over high heat. Add shrimp and cook 2 to 3 minutes or until no longer translucent. Do not overcook!

Reduce heat to medium high. Add garlic and crushed red pepper. Cook and stir 1 minute. Add wine and bring to a boil. Add tomatoes, scallions, oregano, and lemon zest. Return to a boil. Season to taste with salt and pepper.

Toss with pasta in a large bowl. Sprinkle with arugula, feta, and pine nuts and toss lightly.

Serve with additional crushed red pepper to really jazz it up!

Makes 6 to 8 servings

pastas & rice dishes

TOMATO VODKA CHICKEN SPAGHETTI

1 lb of your favorite pasta, cooked according to package directions

1 T olive oil

8 oz cremini mushrooms, sliced

½ to 1 t crushed red pepper

1½ lb chicken breast, ground in food processor

1 medium yellow onion, diced

3 garlic cloves, minced

One 28-oz can crushed tomatoes

One 15-oz can diced tomatoes

⅓ c vodka

1 T chicken base (Better Than Bouillon®)

4 T fresh basil, roughly chopped

6 T fresh parsley, roughly chopped, plus some for garnish

Salt and pepper to taste

8 oz fresh mozzarella, cubed

Heat large skillet over high heat. Add olive oil and brown mushrooms and red pepper, stirring occasionally. Add chicken, onion, and garlic. Cook 15 minutes. Add both cans of undrained tomatoes, vodka, and chicken base. Bring to boil then turn down to a simmer for 10 minutes. Add cream and heat moderately through. Add basil and parsley, then salt and pepper to taste. Add cooked pasta to the sauce and stir to coat.

Mound on serving platter and sprinkle with cubed fresh mozzarella and additional parsley.

SEARED SCALLOPS ATOP SQUASH & APRICOT RISOTTO

4 T olive oil

1 to 1 ½ lb. butternut squash, peeled, seeded and diced

4 T butter

1 medium onion, diced

2 1/2 c Arborio rice

1 c dry white wine, heated

½ c coarsely chopped dried apricots

6 c chicken stock, heated

½ c shredded Parmesan cheese

2 to 3 T coarsely chopped fresh sage

Salt and pepper

SCALLOPS

1 large egg white

2 T water

½ c panko crumbs

¼ c Parmesan cheese, grated

½ t salt

¼ t pepper

2 sea scallops per person, connector removed and blotted dry with paper towels

3 T olive oil

In large saucepan, heat 2 tablespoons of olive oil over medium heat. Add squash and cook for 8 minutes or until tender. Remove from skillet and set aside.

Add 3 tablespoons of butter and remaining 2 tablespoons of oil to saucepan. Heat until melted. Add onion and cook for 5 minutes until softened. Add rice and stir for 2 minutes. Add wine and apricots, stirring until wine is absorbed. Gradually ladle in stock, allowing each to absorb before adding more. Stir until all stock is absorbed and rice is tender to the bite and creamy, about 20 minutes. Stir in remaining tablespoon of butter, squash, cheese, and sage. Season to taste with salt and pepper.

For the scallops, in a shallow dish whisk together egg white and water. In another shallow dish, combine panko, Parmesan, salt, and pepper.

Dip tops and bottoms only of each scallop in egg white mixture, then in panko.

In a large skillet, heat oil over medium high heat.

Pan fry until golden brown on each side and heated through. Be careful, scallops are easy to overcook and they become tough.

Serve risotto on plate or in shallow bowl and top with delicious sea scallops. Serve with additional gratings of cheese and cracked pepper. As a finishing touch, zest with lemon and/or garnish with fresh chopped parsley.

Makes 4 to 5 servings

pastas & rice dishes

CHIANTI BOLOGNESE ALLA PAPPARDELLE

3 stalks celery, chopped

1 large onion, chopped

2 large carrots, chopped

4 cloves garlic, thinly sliced

2 T olive oil

3 lb ground beef chuck

2 to 3 oz pancetta, chopped

2 c tomato sauce

1 T beef base (Better Than Bouillon®)

3 c Chianti

¾ c heavy cream

Salt and pepper

1 lb of your favorite pasta

½ c Parmesan cheese (plus additional for serving) grated

½ c fresh basil, coarsely chopped

Cook pasta according to package directions until al dente. Researve ½ cup of the cooking water.

In a food processor, combine first celery, onion, carrots, and garlic. Process to a coarse paste.

In a large skillet, heat oil over medium high heat. Add vegetable mixture and sauté briefly until nicely browned. Add ground beef and pancetta and cook until brown. Add tomato sauce and beef base and cook through. Add Chianti and simmer 10 minutes to cook out alcohol taste. Add cream and return to a simmer. Season to taste with salt and pepper. Add pasta to sauce and toss to coat. Add pasta water and heat through.

Remove from heat. Stir in Parmesan and basil.

Divide the sauced pasta into individual serving bowls or put in one big pasta bowl. Top with more Parmesan and pass around additional Parmesan.

Makes 6 to 8 servings

IOWA CHARRED CORN & JALAPEÑO RISOTTO

2 T butter

1 medium onion, diced

1 small to medium jalapeño pepper, diced

1 T garlic, chopped

1 c Arborio rice

½ c dry white wine, heated

2 c chicken stock, heated

2 ears charred corn over an open flame, corn cut from cob

¼ c fresh Italian flat leaf parsley, coarsely chopped

Salt and pepper

½ c Parmesan cheese, freshly shredded

In large pot, melt butter over medium high heat. Add onion, jalapeño, and garlic. Cook 5 minutes or until tender. Add rice and stir to coat with butter. Add wine, stirring until absorbed. Gradually ladle in stock, allowing each to absorb before adding more. When half of the stock has been incorporated, add the corn. Add parsley and adjust seasoning with salt and pepper.

Garnish with Parmesan and additional parsley.

Makes 4 to 6 servings

pastas & rice dishes

AUTUMN PASTA WITH BUTTERNUT SQUASH PROSCIUTTO SAUCE

2 lb (5 cups) butternut squash, peeled and deseeded, cut in small cubes

Salt and pepper

2 T olive oil

1 c (8 oz) prosciutto, julienned

¾ c shallot, coarsely chopped

1 sprig (6 to 8 leaves) fresh sage

1 c dry white wine

1 c half-and-half

1 c chicken broth

1 lb your choice pasta, cooked as directed

2 c shredded aged Gouda cheese

Italian flat leaf parsley, coarsely chopped

Preheat oven 350°F

In a bowl combine squash, a sprinkling of salt and pepper, and a drizzle of olive oil. Pour out onto a shallow baking pan.

Roast 30 minutes or until golden and tender.

In large skillet, heat 2 tablespoons of olive oil over medium high heat. Add prosciutto, shallot, and sage. Cook until prosciutto is crisp and shallot is tender. Remove from skillet.

Into the skillet, pour the wine and bring to a boil, scraping the bottom of the skillet with a wooden spoon to remove any browned bits. Simmer until it's nearly evaporated then add the half-and-half and broth. Heat through. Add half of roasted squash and blend until smooth with immersion blender or using a blender or food processor (in batches).

Add in prosciutto mixture and the rest of the squash. Season to taste with salt and pepper and toss with pasta. Add most of Gouda.

Pour pasta into serving bowl(s) and garnish with remaining cheese and fresh parsley. Pass with pepper mill and good bread!

Makes 6 to 8 servings

STUFFED PASTA SHELLS

Nonstick cooking spray

20 jumbo pasta shells

1½ to 2 lbs boneless, skinless chicken breast halves

3 T olive oil

3 cloves garlic, minced

2 large eggs

One 15-oz carton part skim ricotta cheese

One 8-oz package cream cheese, softened

½ c Italian cheese (Parmesan, Asiago, or Romano) shredded

1 small red onion, coarsely chopped

½ c sun dried tomatoes

¼ c fresh basil

1 T black pepper

2 t salt

6 cloves garlic, minced

1 T anchovy paste

1½ t crushed red pepper

Four 14.5-oz cans diced tomatoes, undrained

2 c olives (Your choice Greek, black, and/or green. I use all.) coarsely chopped

3 T capers

¾ c Italian flat leaf parsley, coarsely chopped, plus additional for garnish

Salt and pepper

Preheat oven to 350°F. Coat a 13x9-inch baking dish with nonstick spray.

Cook pasta shells for 1 minute less than package directions and rinse in cold water to stop cooking.

In a food processor, pulse chicken to finely grind.

In a large skillet, heat 1 tablespoon of olive oil over medium heat. Add ground chicken and garlic and cook until chicken is no longer pink. Remove from skillet; set aside to cool.

In a food processor, combine eggs and all cheeses. Pulse until puréed. Add onion, tomatoes, basil, pepper, and salt. Pulse to coarsely chop. In a large bowl, combine creamed mixture and cooked chicken mixture.

Use a scoop or spoon to fill each pasta shell. Place filled shells in prepared baking dish. Refrigerate until ready to bake.

In a large saucepan, heat 2 tablespoons of olive oil on medium heat. Add garlic, anchovy paste, and crushed red pepper. Cook and stir 1 minute or until fragrant. Add undrained tomatoes, olives, and capers. Bring to a boil. Reduce heat and simmer uncovered for 20 minutes. Stir in parsley and season to taste with salt and pepper. You won't need much salt, but you will need pepper for sure.

Spoon sauce gently over shells.

Bake for one hour or until it reaches an internal temperature of 160°F.

Garnish with additional parsley and cheese.

Makes 8 servings

LEEK, FENNEL & APRICOT RISOTTO

6 T Butter

½ c fennel bulb, shaved

2 leeks, pale green and white parts, halved lengthwise and cut crosswise into half moons

⅓ c coarsely chopped dried apricots

1 t minced garlic

Salt and pepper

1 c Arborio rice

½ c dry white wine, heated

2 c vegetable stock, heated

1 T fresh parsley, chopped

In a medium to large sauce pan, melt 2 tablespoons of butter over medium high heat. Add fennel, leeks, apricots, and garlic. Cook and stir 5 to 8 minutes until tender. Season to taste with salt and pepper. Remove from pan and set aside.

Melt remaining 4 tablespoons of butter in pan. Add rice and stir to coat. Add wine, stirring until absorbed.

Gradually ladle in stock, stirring until all is absorbed and rice is tender and creamy. Add reserved vegetable mixture and heat through.

Garnish with parsley.

Makes 4 to 6 servings

TERRIE'S TIDBIT

Risotto is one of my favorite things. It's so comforting. It's a labor of love, standing there and stirring for 20 minutes.

ITALIAN SAUSAGE & ARUGULA PASTA

¼ c olive oil

1 c yellow onion, chopped

2 T dried basil or ½ c chopped fresh basil

4 cloves garlic, chopped

1½ t ground pepper

1 t oregano

½ t crushed red pepper, ground

Three 14.5-oz cans diced tomatoes

1½ lb Italian sausage, browned

6.5 oz marinated artichoke hearts, drained, reserve marinade

½ c sliced black olives

Salt and pepper

3 to 4 oz arugula

¼ c Italian parsley, chopped

1 lb your choice pasta, cooked according to package directions

Parmesan cheese, grated

In a large skillet, heat oil over medium heat. Add onion, basil, garlic, pepper, oregano, and crushed red pepper. Cook for 5 minutes or until onion soft, careful not burn red pepper. Add tomatoes, sausage, artichoke marinade, and black olives. Simmer uncovered 15 minutes or until flavors meld. Adjust seasoning with salt and pepper.

At the end of cooking, stir in arugula, parsley, and artichokes. Toss with pasta and place in pasta bowl or platter. Pass grated Parmesan around the table.

Makes 6 to 8 servings

THAI "DRUNKEN NOODLES" WITH PLUMP SHRIMP

14-oz package wide rice noodles

3 T peanut oil

2 shallots, thinly sliced

4 cloves garlic, thinly sliced

1-inch piece fresh ginger, minced

1 T chili garlic sauce

1 lb medium shrimp, peeled and deveined

¼ c fish sauce

¼ c soy sauce

¼ c rice vinegar

2 T brown sugar

2 tomatoes, cut in bite size pieces

1 c bean sprouts

1 c bell pepper, thinly sliced

1 lime, juiced

1 bunch fresh cilantro, chopped

1 bunch fresh Thai basil, or sweet basil, chopped

¾ c peanuts, chopped

Hot sauce

Cook noodles in boiling water for 7 to 8 minutes. Drain and set aside.

In a large skillet, heat oil over medium heat. Add shallots, garlic, ginger, and chili sauce. Cook briefly until softened. Add shrimp and sauté briefly. Add fish sauce, soy sauce, vinegar, and brown sugar. Bring to a boil. Add tomatoes, bean sprouts, peppers, and cooked noodles. Cook until heated through. Add lime juice.

Serve portions with cilantro, basil, and peanuts. Pass around the hot sauce!

Makes 4 to 6 servings

ORZO PASTA WITH BACON, OLIVES & FETA

1 T olive oil

1 T butter

3 strips thick-sliced bacon, snipped

1 shallot, minced

1 T garlic, minced

2 c orzo

2 c vegetable stock

Salt and pepper

4 oz (3 c) fresh arugula

¾ c crumbled feta cheese

½ c pine nuts, toasted

½ c Kalamata olives, chopped

2 T fresh parsley, chopped

1 t fresh rosemary, chopped

1 t fresh thyme, chopped

In a medium skillet, heat oil and butter over medium high heat. Add bacon and cook 10 minutes, stirring until crisp. Remove from skillet and drain on paper towels. Add shallot and garlic to rendered bacon fat in skillet and cook briefly to soften. Add orzo and cook 4 to 5 minutes until toasted and flavors are absorbed. Add stock and bring to a boil. Reduce heat and simmer 15 to 20 minutes. Check halfway through cooking and add additional stock if needed. Season to taste with salt and pepper.

Just before serving add arugula, feta, nuts, olives, parsley, rosemary, thyme, and bacon.

Makes 4 to 6 generous servings

pastas & rice dishes

BUTTERNUT SQUASH & ROOT VEGETABLE LASAGNA

2 lbs butternut squash, peeled, seeded and diced into small cubes

1 lb sweet potato, skin on, diced into small cubes

1 lb carrot, skin on, diced

Olive oil

5 c milk

1 c onion, diced

Sprig of fresh sage

1 t each salt and pepper

¼ t freshly grated nutmeg

⅓ c all-purpose flour

1¼ c Parmesan cheese, grated

Nonstick cooking spray

9 no-boil lasagna noodles

2 c smoked Gouda, grated

Fresh sage, Chopped

I created this for a Fall episode of Iowa Ingredient on IPTV.

Preheat oven to 400°F.

In a large bowl, combine squash, sweet potato, and carrot. Drizzle with olive oil and toss to coat. Divide mixture between two sheet pans. Roast 20 minutes or until tender, stirring once after 10 minutes. Remove from oven. Reduce oven temperature to 350°F.

In a large saucepan, combine milk, onion, sage, salt, pepper, and nutmeg. Bring to a simmer over medium heat. Remove sage sprig. Whisk in flour, stirring until thickened. Remove from heat and add Parmesan cheese.

Lightly coat a 13x9-inch baking dish with nonstick spray. Pour in 1 cup of milk mixture. Layer in 3 noodles, half of the squash mixture, ½ cup of Gouda, 1 cup of the milk mixture. Repeat layers twice, ending with the milk mixture. Top with remaining gouda cheese.

Lightly coat a sheet of foil and place sprayed side down on top of the dish. Bake 30 minutes. Uncover and bake 10 more minutes or until hot and bubbly. Let stand 10 minutes before cutting to serve.

Garnish with fresh cut sage.

STRAWBERRY RISOTTO WITH BASIL CHIFFONADE

4 c vegetable stock

1¾ c dry white wine

6 T butter, divided

1½ c arborio rice

¾ c finely chopped red onion

2¾ c strawberries, hulled, plus several whole for garnish

1 c Parmesan cheese, freshly grated

Salt and white pepper

Fresh basil, shredded

Heat stock and wine in separate pots.

In a large pan, melt 3 tablespoons butter over medium heat. Add rice and onion, cook 1 minute to coat rice grains. Add the wine and stir until it is completely absorbed. Add stock ladle by ladle and cook, stirring, until each ladleful is absorbed, about 20 minutes.

Slice strawberries and add to pan about 10 minutes before rice is complete. When it is almost ready, gently stir in cheese and remaining 3 tablespoons butter. Season to taste with salt and white pepper.

Serve garnished with the reserved whole strawberries and basil.

Makes 6 to 8 servings

pastas & rice dishes

I want to empower people to switch out ingredients and make substitutions when necessary (or for fun!). If you don't have sherry vinegar, use balsamic. If you don't have pork chops, use chicken breasts. If you don't like bananas and walnuts, use cherries and almonds.

meaty mains

98	STUFFED IOWA PORK CHOPS
99	MOROCCAN CHICKEN STEW OVER JUMBO COUSCOUS
100	ANDOUILLE & CHICKEN JAMBALAYA
101	SPICE RUBBED LAMB CHOPS WITH CUCUMBER MINT SAUCE
102	SOUTHWESTERN MARGUERITA CHICKEN SKEWERS
103	CORNBREAD STUFFED ROASTED TURKEY BREAST WITH CIDER SAUCE
104	CHICKEN CACCIATORE
105	STUFFED BEEF TOURNEDO WITH MERLOT MUSTARD SAUCE
106	MAPLE BACON WRAPPED PORK TENDERLOIN WITH ROSEMARY CHERRY SAUCE
107	SWEET & SOUR CHICKEN OR PORK
108	TUSCAN CHICKEN SPIEDINI WITH AMOGIO SAUCE
109	ESPRESSO AND CHILI RUBBED FLANK STEAK
110	CHICKEN MARSALA
111	FRENCH PORK MEDALLIONS WITH LAVENDER & GRAPES
112	STEAK OSCAR WITH BÉARNAISE
113	PROVENCAL CHICKEN BREASTS WITH HERBES DE PROVENCE ORZO
114	CHICKEN PICCATA WITH LEMON CAPER SAUCE
115	COFFEE CRUSTED TENDERLOIN WITH RED WINE JUS
116	CHICKEN ROLLATINI
117	BEEF TENDERLOIN WITH JAZZY RED PEPPER SAUCE
118	ROMANTIC DUET OF CHICKEN IN PORT CHERRY SAUCE

STUFFED IOWA PORK CHOPS

8 bone-in pork loin chops, cut 1¼ to 1½-inch thick. 6 to 8 oz each

Salt and pepper

Olive oil

1 recipe Apple Sage Stuffing (page 136)

OR

1 recipe Apple Walnut Bacon Stuffing (page 137)

In most stuffed pork chop recipes, or chicken breast or beef medallions, the instructions say to make the slit in the meat, stuff it, put a toothpick in, and bake it. I brown it first, then make the slit, stuff, and bake. This way, the meat is sturdy so you can make a nice slit and the stuffing stays in much better!

Preheat oven to 350°F. Line a sheet pan with parchment paper. Set aside.

Let chops stand at room temperature for 20 minutes prior to preparation. Pat chops dry with a paper towel. Season with salt and pepper.

In a skillet, heat oil over medium high to high heat. Sear pork chops on each side 4 minutes or so, but do not cook through. Careful not to crowd the pan – cook in batches if necessary.

Use a long thin knife to cut a horizontal pocket in the side of each chop. Use stuffing of choice to evenly fill all 8 pockets.

Place chops on prepared sheet pan. Bake 15 to 25 minutes until just pink in the center or until an instant-read thermometer inserted in the center reads 145°F.

MOROCCAN CHICKEN STEW OVER JUMBO COUSCOUS

1 to 2 T olive oil

2 lbs ground chicken

2 onions, chopped

2 large garlic cloves, thinly sliced

1 t ground cinnamon

1 t ground ginger

½ t saffron threads

¼ t cayenne pepper

1 c chicken stock or broth

One 15-oz can garbanzo beans

One 14.5-oz can diced tomatoes

1 green bell pepper, finely chopped

1 medium carrot, finely chopped

⅓ c golden raisins

2 T cold water

2 T cornstarch

Salt and pepper

Jumbo Israeli couscous, cooked according to package directions

Slivered almond, toasted

Fresh parsley, chopped

In a large pot, heat oil over medium high heat. Add chicken, onions, and garlic. Stir until chicken is broken up and no longer pink and onion is tender. Add cinnamon, ginger, saffron, and cayenne. Stir 1 minute or until fragrant. Add the stock or broth, garbanzo beans, tomatoes, bell pepper, carrot, and raisins. Bring to a boil. Reduce heat and simmer 10 to 15 minutes or until vegetables are tender.

In a small bowl, whisk together water and cornstarch to make a slurry. Add gradually to the pot, stirring constantly. Continue to cook and stir until thickened and bubbly. Season to taste with salt and pepper.

Serve over couscous. Garnish with toasted slivered almonds and fresh parsley.

Makes 6 to 8 servings

meaty mains

ANDOUILLE & CHICKEN JAMBALAYA

3 T butter

1 large red onion, chopped

1 medium green pepper, chopped

1 stalk celery, chopped

1 clove garlic, thinly sliced

1 T Cajun seasoning

1 lb chicken breast, trimmed and cut into bite size pieces

14 oz Andouille sausage, cut diagonally

2 c uncooked white rice

One 15-oz can diced tomatoes, do not drain

1 T tomato paste

1 t Worcestershire sauce

1 t dried oregano

1 c frozen okra

3 c hot chicken broth

Salt and pepper

Fresh parsley for garnish

In a large saucepan, melt butter over low heat. Turn up to medium heat and stir in onion, pepper, celery, garlic, Cajun seasoning, chicken, and sausage. Cook, stirring, until onion is soft. Add rice and stir to coat, several minutes. Stir in tomatoes with liquid from can, tomato paste, Worcestershire sauce, oregano, okra, and broth. Cover and simmer until just a little liquid remains, about 20 minutes. Season to taste.

Spoon out onto platter and garnish with fresh parsley. Pass the Louisiana Hot Sauce!

SPICE RUBBED LAMB CHOPS WITH CUCUMBER MINT SAUCE

1 t paprika

1 t granulated garlic

1 t kosher salt

1 t black pepper

1 t ground rosemary

2 lbs Frenched rack of lamb or 6 lamb chop loins cut 1¼-inch thick, room temperature

SAUCE

½ c sour cream

⅓ c fresh mint leaves, chopped

3 T English cucumber, peeled, seeded, and chopped

½ t lemon juice

½ t garlic, minced

¼ t white pepper

¼ t kosher salt

The secret to lamb is preparing it properly. If you just eat a lamb chop it's going to taste gamey. You need something to counter the taste, but not make it completely go away.
This dish can also be prepared as an appetizer – just call them "lamb-sicles."

Preheat oven to 375°F. Line a sheet pan with parchment paper.

To prepare Mint Sauce, stir all ingredients together and refrigerate until needed.

For lamb rub, combine paprika, garlic, salt, pepper, and rosemary and put in shaker.

Preheat a grill pan or ovensafe skillet over high heat.

Trim any silverskin from lamb. Rinse and pat dry with paper towels. If using rack of lamb, cut between bones to make into "riblets."

Season one side of "riblet" or loin, place seasoned side down in hot grill pan. Do not move, cook 2 to 3 minutes to get grill marks. Season other side, turn and cook 2 to 3 minutes to mark the other side.

Place lamb on prepared pan and bake for 5 to 10 minutes or to 145°F degrees on instant-read thermometer.

Serve with Cucumber Mint Sauce.

Makes 4 to 6 servings

meaty mains

SOUTHWESTERN MARGUERITA CHICKEN SKEWERS

zest of 1 lime

¾ c lime juice

½ c tequila

½ c honey

¼ c canola oil

2 to 3 cloves garlic, thinly sliced

1 t each salt and pepper

1 t ground cumin

2 lbs boneless skinless chicken breast halves, trimmed, rinsed, and cut into bite-size cubes

1 T cornstarch

1 T cold water

Eight 12-inch bamboo or metal skewers

Lime wedges

For marinade, in a medium bowl combine lime zest, juice, tequila, honey, oil, garlic, salt, pepper, and cumin. Place chicken in a resealable plastic bag and set in a shallow dish. Pour 2/3 cup of the marinade mixture over the chicken. Reserve the remaining marinade. Marinate chicken in the refrigerator 2 hours up to overnight. Drain and discard used marinade.

In a small saucepan, bring the reserved marinade mixture to a boil. Whisk together cornstarch and water. Drizzle into boiling sauce while stirring. Allow to come back to a boil, then cover and set aside or refrigerate.

Soak wood skewers in water at least 30 minutes before grilling.

Preheat an outdoor grill to medium heat.

Thread chicken on skewers, not too tight. Place skewers on a pan sprayed grill rack. Cover and grill until grill marks form on each side.

Baste with marinade sauce on each side and continue grilling until cooked through and no longer pink, 160°F.

Garnish with lime wedges.

Makes 4 to 6 servings

CORNBREAD STUFFED ROASTED TURKEY BREAST WITH CIDER SAUCE

One 8.5-oz Jiffy® corn muffin mix

2 T butter

1 medium red onion, diced

1 stalk celery, diced

3 cloves garlic, diced

1 egg, lightly beaten

1½ t dried sage

1 t salt

1½ t pepper

1 t dried thyme

1½ - 2½ c chicken stock

2 c of preferred add-ins: dried fruit, chestnuts, nuts

One 6-lb turkey breast, skin retained, deboned, and butterflied into thirds (slice through a third of the breast, open and slice through the 2/3 side to open like a book)

Granulated garlic

Paprika

1 recipe Cider Sauce (page 138)

This is one of my earliest recipes. I created it while I was in culinary school. I am a white meat turkey lover, and I created this recipe because I love cornbread, too.

Preheat oven to 300°F.

Prepare muffin mix according to package directions to make cornbread. Cool and crumble. Spread on a sheet pan and bake for 10 to 15 minutes, stirring every 5 minutes. Loosely cover the sheet pan with a kitchen towel and let stand overnight.

Preheat oven to 350°F

In medium skillet, heat butter over medium high heat and cook onion, celery, and garlic until tender.

In a large bowl, combine the egg, sage, salt, pepper, and thyme. Add dried cornbread, cooked vegetable mixture, and enough stock to moisten the mixture. Add dried fruit, and/or chestnuts, if desired.

Spread stuffing onto turkey breast, roll up (side to side) and tie off using 100% cotton kitchen string.

Sprinkle liberally with additional salt, pepper, granulated garlic, and paprika.

Place a rack in a roasting pan. Set turkey roll on the rack. Roast 75 minutes or until an instant-read thermometer reads 160°F. Let rest 10 minutes before slicing.

Remove strings, slice, and place on serving platter or individual plates. Top with sauce. Delish!

Makes 4 to 6 servings

CHICKEN CACCIATORE

2 lbs skinless boneless chicken breast halves, trimmed and cut into strips

Salt and pepper

2 T butter

2 T olive oil

3 medium bell peppers (red, yellow, orange or green), julienned

1 large red onion, julienned

1 large fennel bulb, julienned

½ c olives (black, green, and/or Kalamata), coarsely chopped

4 cloves garlic, sliced

Two 14.5-oz. cans diced tomatoes, undrained

2 to 3 lemons, juiced and zested

1 T chicken base (Better Than Bouillon®)

1 T capers

1 to 3 t crushed red pepper

2 T cornstarch

Fresh parsley, chopped

Season chicken with salt and pepper. In a large skillet, heat butter and oil over medium high heat. Add chicken and sear on either side until golden brown. Transfer chicken from skillet to a platter.

Add bell peppers, onion, fennel, olives, and garlic to skillet, adding additional butter or oil if needed. Cook 5 to 8 minutes until crisp-tender.

Add undrained tomatoes, 1 cup water, lemon juice and zest, chicken base, capers, and crushed red pepper. Bring to a boil.

Whisk together cornstarch and 2 tablespoons of water. Stir mixture into the skillet, stirring constantly until thickened and bubbly.

Add chicken and juices back into the skillet and heat through. Season to taste with salt and pepper.

Garnish with parsley.

Makes 6 to 8 servings

STUFFED BEEF TOURNEDO WITH MERLOT MUSTARD SAUCE

2 T olive oil

2 T butter

Four 5 to 6-oz beef tournedo steaks

Salt

Black pepper, coarsely ground

½ c bleu cheese crumbles

½ c toasted walnuts, chopped

1 c red wine

1 c beef broth

2 T Dijon mustard

2 T cold butter

2 T cornstarch

Preheat oven to 400°F. Line sheetpan with parchment paper.

In a large skillet, heat olive oil and butter over high heat. Season the tournedos with salt and pepper on each side. Place them into the skillet and sear each side until golden brown. May need to do in batches so as not to steam them. Remove the steaks to the sheetpan. Make a horizontal slit in the side of each steak and stuff each with bleu cheese and walnuts.

Bake steaks in oven until 145°F when tested with an instant-read thermometer.

Quickly make sauce in the skillet while steaks are baking. Remove all but 3 tablespoons of the fat from the pan and return to high heat. Add the red wine and simmer until reduced by half. Add the broth and simmer until reduced by half. Whisk in the mustard and butter and cook for 30 seconds. In a small bowl whisk together cornstarch and 2 tablespoons cold water. Whisk cornstarch mixture into the sauce mixture. Simmer while whisking until thickened and bubbly. Season to taste with salt and pepper.

Serve each fillet on a plate and lightly coat with sauce.

Makes 4 servings

meaty mains

MAPLE BACON WRAPPED PORK TENDERLOIN WITH ROSEMARY CHERRY SAUCE

Two 2-lb pork tenderloins, silverskin trimmed

1½ lbs maple bacon

Olive oil

1 c red onion, julienned

¾ c dried cherries

2 t garlic, minced

2 t fresh rosemary, chopped or 1 t dried rosemary, crushed

1½ c chicken stock

1 T red wine vinegar

1 T cornstarch

I did a segment about cherries on IPTV's culinary series "Iowa Ingredient" with Charity Nebbe. I prepared this dish along with a cherry upside-down cake.

Preheat oven to 375°F. Line sheet pan with parchment paper.

Spiral wrap pork tenderloins with bacon and secure with toothpicks.

In a large skillet, heat 1 tablespoon olive oil over high heat. Add tenderloins to skillet and sear on all four sides, not cooking through. Transfer to sheet pan. Bake about 20 minutes until instant-read thermometer reads 145°F.

Meanwhile, in same skillet heat 1 teaspoon olive oil on medium high heat. Add onion, dried cherries, garlic, and rosemary. Cook 10 minutes or until onions are golden. Add chicken stock and scrape bottom to de-glaze. Turn heat to high and bring to a boil.

Whisk together vinegar and cornstarch. Gradually add mixture to pan, whisking continuously until sauce is thickened and bubbly, about 1 minute.

Remove pan from heat, cover, and set aside until serving. If sauce cools, warm in pan, covered, over low heat. If it thickens, use whisk in a few tablespoons chicken broth.

Makes 6 to 8 servings

TERRIE'S TIDBIT

Chicken breast works beautifully in the recipe as well.

SWEET & SOUR CHICKEN OR PORK

1 c oil

4 whole chicken breasts (or equal amount of pork), skinned, boned, cut into 1-inch chunks

½ t salt

1 egg, beaten

¾ c biscuit mix

⅔ c sugar

2 T cornstarch

1 T paprika

One 20-oz can pineapple chunks

½ c soy sauce

¼ c cider vinegar

1 c green bell pepper, cut into strips

½ c onion, sliced

2 medium tomatoes, chopped

Hot cooked rice

This recipe goes back to the 70s and may it remind you of The Dragon restaurant in Cedar Rapids, Iowa.

Heat oil in a heavy medium saucepan to 400°F. Preheat oven to 200°F.

Sprinkle chicken with salt. Place egg in a shallow dish. Place biscuit mix in a second shallow dish. Dip chicken pieces in egg, then in biscuit mix to coat.

Fry chicken in batches in hot oil, turning, until just brown and crisp. Remove from saucepan and drain on paper towels. Place in oven to keep warm.

In a 10-inch skillet, combine sugar, cornstarch, and paprika. Drain pineapple and add enough water to the pineapple juice to make 2 cups. Add juice, soy sauce, and vinegar to cornstarch mixture. Cook over medium heat, stirring constantly, until mixture comes to a boil. Boil 1 minute. Add green pepper and onion. Cover and cook 5 minutes until crisp-tender. Add pineapple and tomatoes, heat through. Stir in chicken.

Serve over rice.

Makes 6 to 8 servings

meaty mains

TUSCAN CHICKEN SPIEDINI WITH AMOGIO SAUCE

½ c all-purpose flour

1 t each salt and pepper

2 eggs, lightly beaten

2 T Dijon mustard

2 t lemon zest

1 c panko crumbs

½ c Parmesan cheese, grated

2 t Italian seasoning

1 t granulated garlic

Eight 5-oz boneless skinless chicken breast halves

3 T olive oil

3 T butter

SAUCE

½ c olive oil

½ c butter

3 cloves garlic, minced

½ t crushed red pepper

¼ c lemon juice

1 T chopped fresh parsley

Salt and pepper

You may associate this dish with Latin King restaurant in Des Moines. I've simplified the preparation to make it more approachable for the home kitchen.

Preheat oven to 350°F. Line a sheet pan with parchment paper.

In a shallow dish, combine flour, pepper and salt. In a second shallow dish combine eggs, mustard, and lemon zest. In a third shallow dish combine panko, Parmesan, Italian seasoning, and garlic. Dredge chicken first in the flour mixture, then in the egg mixture, and finally in the panko mixture to coat.

In a large skillet over medium high heat add oil and butter. Add chicken in batches and cook 4 to 5 minutes until nicely crisp and brown on both sides. Do not cook through. Transfer chicken to the prepared pan. Bake 10 to 15 minutes until 160°F when tested with an instant-read thermometer.

For the sauce, in the same skillet used to brown the chicken, heat oil and butter over medium high heat. Add garlic and crushed red pepper and cook 1 minute or until fragrant. Add lemon juice and parsley. Heat through. Season to taste with salt and pepper.

Ladle sauce over chicken to serve.

Makes 8 servings

ESPRESSO AND CHILI RUBBED FLANK STEAK

1½ t chili powder

1½ t instant espresso coffee powder

½ t brown sugar

½ t granulated garlic

¼ t dry mustard

¼ t ground cumin

¼ t each salt and pepper

1½ lbs beef flank steak

Olive oil

1 recipe Poblano Pesto (page 141)

Preheat oven to 350°F.

Combine chili powder, coffee powder, brown sugar, garlic, mustard, cumin, salt, and pepper. Coat the steak well with the rub mixture on both sides.

Heat a large ovensafe skillet over medium high heat. Add enough olive oil just to cover the bottom of the skillet. Sear steak on either side until golden brown, not cooking through. Move to the oven and bake 10 minutes or until temperature reads 145°F (for medium-rare).

Thinly slice steak and serve with Poblano Pesto.

Makes 4 servings

CHICKEN MARSALA

½ c all-purpose flour

1 t each salt and pepper

¼ cup olive oil

¼ cup butter

4 boneless, skinless chicken breast halves (about 1½ lbs) trimmed, if thick, butterfly (slice through a third of the breast, open and slice through the 2/3 side to open like a book)

8 oz cremini mushrooms, rinsed clean and sliced

½ red onion, julienned

1 to 2 cloves garlic, thinly sliced

¾ c sweet Marsala wine

¾ c chicken stock

2 T butter

¼ c flat-leaf parsley, coarsely chopped

This dish is delightful served over pasta.

Preheat oven to 350°F. Line a baking sheet with parchment paper.

In a large skillet, heat olive oil and butter over medium high heat.

In a shallow platter, stir together flour, salt and pepper. Dredge both sides of the chicken in seasoned flour, shaking off the excess. Place chicken in the skillet and sear both sides, do not cook through. Place on prepared baking sheet. Bake until an instant-read thermometer inserted into the center reads 160°F.

Add the mushrooms, onion, and garlic to the skillet. Cook 5 minutes or until nicely browned and moisture has evaporated. Carefully pour in the Marsala. Bring to a boil and cook for a few seconds to cook out the alcohol. Add the chicken stock. Return to a boil. Simmer for 1 minute to reduce the sauce slightly. Stir in the butter. Adjust the seasoning with salt and pepper. Return the chicken to the pan and simmer gently for 1 or 2 minutes to heat the chicken through.

Garnish with chopped parsley before serving.

Makes 4 servings

FRENCH PORK MEDALLIONS WITH LAVENDER & GRAPES

Two 2-lb pork tenderloins

1 c all-purpose flour

1 T herbes de Provence

1 t each salt and pepper

1 t lavender

Olive oil

2 T butter

½ c red onion, thinly julienned

4 cloves garlic, thinly sliced

1½ c water

½ c dry white wine

2 t chicken base (Better Than Bouillon®)

2 T cornstarch

2 T cold water

1 c red grapes, halved

Italian flat leaf parsley, coarsely chopped

Herbes de Provence is a mixture of basil, fennel seed, lavender, marjoram, rosemary, sage, summer savory and thyme. It is most commonly used in southern France.

Preheat oven to 350°F. Line a sheet pan with parchment paper.

Trim silverskin from tenderloins, cut crosswise into 2-inch portions. In a shallow dish, combine flour, herbes de Provence, salt, pepper, and lavender. Dredge pork in flour mixture to coat.

In a large skillet, heat 2 tablespoons olive oil and butter. Add pork in batches to brown on both sides. Do not crowd pan. Transfer to sheet pan and bake 10 minutes to finish cooking to 145°F.

Add ¼ cup olive oil to skillet and heat on medium high. Add onion and garlic and cook 6 minutes until tender.

Add water, wine, and base. Bring to a boil, stirring with a wooden spoon to release any browned bits from the bottom of the skillet.

Whisk together cornstarch and cold water. Slowly drizzle into sauce, stirring constantly so as not to create lumps. Cook and stir until thickened and bubbly. Add grapes and heat through.

Serve medallions on platter. Lightly coat with sauce and garnish with parsley.

Makes 8 servings

STEAK OSCAR WITH BÉARNAISE

12 to 18 asparagus spears

Six 5-oz beef tenderloin medallions

Salt and pepper

2 T butter

2 T olive oil

1 lb lump crabmeat

SAUCE

2 T butter

1 to 2 shallots, chopped

1 T fresh tarragon, chopped

1 T fresh chives, chopped

Zest of 1 lemon

Preheat oven to 375°F.

In a large saucepan, bring a small amount of water to a boil. Add a steamer insert and place in asparagus. Cover and steam 3 minutes or until tender. Remove from steamer and keep warm.

Season tenderloin medallions with salt and pepper. In an ovensafe skillet, heat butter and oil over medium high heat. Add medallions and sear each side. Transfer to oven and bake until an instant-read thermometer inserted in through the side of a medallion reads 145°F. Remove medallions from skillet and tent lightly with foil.

To the pan drippings in the skillet melt butter for the sauce. Stir in shallots, herbs, and zest, stirring to scrape up browned bits from the bottom.

To serve, on each plate place a beef medallion, 2 to 3 asparagus spears, crabmeat, and a drizzle of sauce.

Makes 6 servings

PROVENCAL CHICKEN BREASTS WITH HERBES DE PROVENCE ORZO

2 T olive oil

Eight 5-oz boneless skinless chicken breast halves, trimmed

Salt and pepper

½ c dry white wine

One 28-oz can stewed tomatoes

2½ c chicken stock

4 leeks, white part only, cut in half-moons, rinsed and dried

2 cloves garlic, minced

1 t orange zest

1 c drained, pitted kalamata olives

½ T butter

¾ c orzo

¾ c water

2 t lemon juice

½ t herbes de Provence

In a large skillet, heat oil over medium high heat. Season chicken with salt and pepper and place in skillet, in batches. Brown on both sides then transfer to a platter.

Add wine to skillet and boil, using a wooden spoon to scrape up browned bits in the bottom of the skillet. Cook until almost all the wine is evaporated. Add tomatoes, 2 cups chicken stock, leeks, garlic, and zest. Place chicken along with any juices back in the skillet. Bring to a boil. Reduce heat and simmer covered for 15 minutes or until chicken is no longer pink (160°F), turning once halfway through cooking. Transfer chicken to a heated platter.

Add olives to tomato mixture and boil until slightly thickened. Season to taste with salt and pepper.

In a small saucepan, melt butter over medium high heat. Add orzo. Cook and stir 5 minutes until lightly browned. Stir in water, lemon juice, herbes de Provence, and ¼ teaspoon salt. Bring to a boil, cover and reduce heat to low. Cook 15 minutes or until liquid is absorbed. Remove from heat and let stand, covered, 5 minutes.

Serve chicken over orzo.

Makes 8 servings

meaty mains

CHICKEN PICCATA WITH LEMON CAPER SAUCE

1 c all-purpose flour

1 t salt

½ t black pepper

3 eggs

¼ c Dijon mustard

1 c panko crumbs

¼ c Parmesan cheese, grated

1 T granulated garlic

⅓ c olive oil

6 chicken breasts, boned, skinned and sliced in half if too thick, trimmed

1½ c chicken broth

½ c lemon juice

⅓ c capers, drained

¼ c dry white wine

2 T cornstarch

2 T water

½ c fresh parsley, chopped

In a shallow dish, combine flour, salt, and pepper. In a second shallow dish, whisk together eggs and mustard. In a third shallow dish, combine panko, Parmesan, and garlic. Lightly dredge chicken breasts first in flour mixture, then in the egg mixture, and next in the crumb mixture to coat.

In a large skillet, heat oil over high heat. Place breaded chicken into the skillet, in batches if needed. Do not crowd. Sear chicken 3 minutes on each side or until browned and no longer pink (160°F). Transfer chicken to a platter and keep warm.

Drain excess oil from skillet. Add broth, lemon juice, capers, wine, and ¾ teaspoon salt. Bring to a boil. Use a wooden spoon to scrape up browned bits from the bottom of the skillet.

Combine cornstarch and water to form a thickening slurry. Slowly add to boiling liquid, stirring continuously until thickened and bubbly. Add most of the parsley.

Spoon sauce over chicken. Garnish with remaining parsley.

Makes 6 servings

COFFEE CRUSTED TENDERLOIN WITH RED WINE JUS

One 3-lb beef tenderloin, at room temperature, trimmed

3 T instant espresso coffee

3 T brown sugar

2 t kosher salt

1 t ground cumin

¼ t cayenne pepper

4 T butter, divided

1 c dry red wine

2 c beef stock

Salt and pepper

2 T cornstarch

2 T red wine vinegar

Fresh flat leaf parsley, coarsely chopped

This dish is sturdy and robust. It's so rich and delicious. The cumin really makes it pop.

Preheat oven to 400 F.

In a small bowl, combine coffee, sugar, salt, cumin, and cayenne pepper. Rub mixture all over the tenderloin. With 100% cotton kitchen string, tie the tenderloin crosswise in 2-inch intervals. Trim off excess string.

Place a roasting pan over medium high heat. Melt 2 tablespoons of butter in the pan, then place in the beef. Brown for 1 minute on one side. Add the remaining butter and finish browning on all sides. Move the roasting pan to the oven for 15 minutes or until beef is 145°F (for medium-rare). Transfer tenderloin to a cutting board and tent lightly with foil. Let stand 10 minutes.

To make the jus, pour the red wine into the roasting pan and place it over medium heat. Use a wooden spoon to scrape up any browned bits from the bottom of the pan. Allow the wine to cook until reduced by half, about 5 minutes. Add in the beef stock. Stir to combine, then reduce by half again, about 8 minutes, stirring frequently. Add salt and pepper to taste.

Whisk together cornstarch and vinegar to make a slurry. While jus is boiling, gradually stir in the slurry. Stir until thickened and bubbly.

Remove the twine from the tenderloin and slice. Serve with the jus. Garnish with parsley.

Makes 4 to 6 servings

meaty mains

CHICKEN ROLLATINI

1 lemon, juiced

1 T olive oil

Fresh pepper

½ c panko crumbs

¼ c Parmesan cheese, grated

1 t Italian seasoning

1 t granulated garlic

8 thin chicken cutlets, 3 oz each, blotted dry with paper towels

Four 2.8-oz slices prosciutto, sliced in half

4 slices provolone or mozzarella cheese, sliced in half

1 c fresh spinach

Olive oil nonstick cooking spray

Preheat oven to 450°F.

In a shallow dish, combine lemon juice, olive oil, and pepper. In another shallow dish, combine panko, Parmesan, Italian seasoning, and garlic. Dip the chicken in the lemon-oil mixture, then in the breadcrumb mixture to coat well. Place each cutlet on a work surface. Lay a half slice of prosciutto, half slice of cheese, and some spinach on one side of the chicken cutlet. Roll from a short side and place seam side down in a 9x13 baking dish. When finished, top with remaining crumbs and coat lightly with oil spray.

Bake 25 to 30 minutes or until 160°F when tested with an instant-read thermometer.

Best when served immediately.

Makes 8 servings

BEEF TENDERLOIN WITH JAZZY RED PEPPER SAUCE

¾ t chili powder

½ t garlic powder

½ t black pepper

¼ t salt

¼ t dried oregano

¼ t cumin

Four 5-oz beef tenderloin steaks, cut 1-inch thick, trimmed

2 T olive oil

½ c beef broth

¼ c balsamic vinegar

2 T jalapeño pepper jelly

1 T cornstarch

1 T cold water

Chicken breasts or pork chops also work nicely in this recipe.

Preheat oven to 375°F.

In a shallow dish, combine chili powder, garlic powder, pepper, salt, oregano, and cumin.

Use 100% cotton kitchen string to tie around the perimeter of each steak. This will help them hold their shape as they cook. Place each steak in the spice mix and blot the mixture on each side.

In a large ovensafe skillet, heat oil over medium high heat. Add steaks and get a nice brown sear on both sides.

Transfer to oven to finish cooking to 145°F (for medium rare). Remove beef from skillet and tent lightly with foil for 10 minutes.

Add broth, vinegar, and jelly to the skillet and stir over medium high until melted.

Whisk together cornstarch and water to make a "slurry". Gradually add to hot liquid, stirring constantly until thickened and bubbly.

Remove string from steaks and spoon sauce over them.

Makes 4 servings

meaty mains

ROMANTIC DUET OF CHICKEN IN PORT CHERRY SAUCE

2 T olive oil

8 skinless boneless chicken breasts, trimmed and blotted dry

Salt and pepper

1 red onion, thinly julienned

2 cloves garlic, thinly sliced

1 c port wine

2 c chicken broth

¾ c dried cherries

1 t dry mustard

½ t dried thyme

2 T cornstarch

2 T white balsamic vinegar

Hot cooked white and wild rice mix (optional)

Preheat oven to 375°F. Line a sheet pan with parchment paper.

In a large skillet, heat oil over medium high heat. Sprinkle chicken with salt and pepper. Half at a time, nicely brown each side of breast. Do not cook through. Transfer chicken to the prepared pan. Bake 10 to 15 minutes until no longer pink, 160°F when tested with an instant-read thermometer.

In the same skillet, cook onion and garlic in the pan drippings for 5 to 10 minutes, until tender. Carefully add port and stir up chicken bits. Bring to a boil. Reduce heat to and simmer uncovered until reduced by half. Add broth, cherries, mustard, and thyme. Bring to a boil.

Whisk together cornstarch and vinegar. Gradually stir into boiling mixture, may not need it all. Turn down heat once desired thickness is attained.

Serve Port Cherry Sauce over roasted chicken breasts. May serve with White and Wild Rice mix.

Makes 8 servings

"Dining in is the new eating out!"
MY LONG-TIME MANTRA

My mission is to de-mystify home cooking. When I create my recipes, I try to make them always family-friendly, use ingredients that are found locally, and make it so they are completed in two hours or less.

seafood mains

122   BAKED SALMON EN PAPILLOTE

123   CRISPY SEA SCALLOPS ON BLACK RICE WITH CHILI GARLIC SAUCE

124   STUFFED & BAKED TILAPIA DRAPED IN A LEMON MORNAY SAUCE

125   ORANGE ROUGHY ALLA PUTTANESCA SAUCE

126   *ON THE BACK COVER*
CIDER HERB SALMON FILLET OVER BLACK & ORANGE RICE

127   SHRIMP AND CRISPY BACON OVER CHEESY GRITS

128   GRILLED HALIBUT

BAKED SALMON EN PAPILLOTE

Eight 4 to 5-oz salmon fillets, skin off or on, no thicker than 1 inch

Nonstick cooking spray

1 recipe Spinach Pesto (page 133) (optional)

Fresh vegetables of choice: bell pepper, carrot, zucchini, summer squash, julienned, about ¼ cup per person

Salt and pepper

8 Lemon slices

8 Dill sprigs

⅓ c dry white wine, split between 8 servings

When it's done and you open the paper, the steam assaults your senses – it is so aromatic and beautiful.

Preheat oven to 425°F.

Fold a sheet of parchment paper in half. Cut it so it forms a heart shape when opened. Make it large enough to hold all the ingredients, plus two extra inches.

Coat salmon with nonstick spray and place in the middle of one half of the heart, about an inch from the fold.

Layer on a spreading of Spinach Pesto (optional), vegetables, salt and pepper, lemon slice, dill sprig, then wine.

Fold the heart closed and seal the edges. Start at the top and fold over every inch, twisting under at the bottom.

Place on sheet pan and bake 12 to 15 minutes.

To serve, slide a packet onto each plate and carefully cut an "X" to release steam.

Makes 8 servings

CRISPY SEA SCALLOPS ON BLACK RICE WITH CHILI GARLIC SAUCE

AROMATIC BLACK RICE

2 c water

1 c black rice

½ t salt

Sesame oil

¾ c onion, julienned

2 T fresh ginger, minced

3 cloves garlic, sliced

2 T tamari

Salt and pepper

SCALLOPS

3 egg whites

¼ c cornstarch

1 c panko bread crumbs

1 t each salt and pepper

1 t granulated garlic

1 to 1¼ lb sea scallops (typically 15 scallops per pound), remove muscle (if not already) rinse and pat dry with paper towels

2 t butter

2 t olive oil

1 recipe Chili Garlic Sauce (page 123)

To cook rice, in a medium saucepan combine water, rice, and salt. Bring to a boil. Reduce heat, cover and simmer 30 minutes or until water is absorbed and rice is tender.

In a medium skillet, heat a small amount of sesame oil over medium high heat. Add onion, ginger, and garlic and cook 5 minutes or until translucent. Add mixture to rice along with tamari and 2 tablespoons of sesame oil. Season to taste with salt and pepper.

For the scallops, whisk together egg whites and cornstarch in a shallow dish. In a second shallow dish, combine panko, salt, pepper, and garlic. Dip scallops first in egg white mixture, then in crumb mixture to coat.

In a large skillet, heat butter and oil over medium high heat. Place scallops in skillet, careful not to crowd them, or they will steam rather than sear. Sear 1½ minutes on each side or until golden and crisp.

Serve scallops atop rice and drizzle with Chili Garlic Sauce.

Makes 4 to 6 servings

STUFFED & BAKED TILAPIA DRAPED IN A LEMON MORNAY SAUCE

½ c artichoke hearts

⅓ c roasted red pepper

⅓ c kalamata olives

2 scallions, green parts only

1 T fresh oregano

1½ t garlic, minced

1 t pepper

½ t salt

½ c fontina or Swiss cheese, shredded

Eight 4-oz tilapia fillets

1 t granulated garlic

1 t Paprika

1 recipe Lemon Mornay Sauce (page 145)

Preheat oven to 375°F. Line a sheet pan with parchment paper.

In a food processor, combine artichoke hearts, red pepper, olives, scallions, oregano, garlic, and salt. Pulse briefly just to chop. Place in medium bowl and stir in cheese.

Lay tilapia on prepared sheet pan. Place even amount of artichoke mixture on bottom half of each fillet. Fold fish in half and sprinkle with garlic and paprika. Place in oven and bake until an instant-read thermometer reads 145°F. This won't take long as fish cooks quickly.

Place tilapia on a serving plate, coat with Lemon Mornay Sauce and garnish with chopped parsley.

Makes 8 servings

ORANGE ROUGHY ALLA PUTTANESCA SAUCE

2 lbs orange roughy fillets

Salt and pepper

Olive oil

2 T butter

5 to 10 cloves garlic, minced

1 t crushed red pepper

1 T anchovy paste

Four 14.5-oz cans diced Italian tomatoes, drained saving 1 c juice

12 to 15 brine-cured black olives, coarsely chopped

2 T capers

½ c Italian parsley, chopped, divided

Salt and pepper

Parmesan cheese, freshly grated

This recipe is great with any fish – chicken, too.

Season fish fillets with salt and pepper on presentation side.

Heat a large skillet over medium high heat. Add 2 tablespoons of olive oil and the butter. When hot and melted, add fillets to skillet, presentation side down.

Depending on thickness of fillet, turn when golden brown, then turn again when golden brown. A good rule of thumb is 4 to 6 minutes per ½-inch of thickness until fish just flakes when tested with a fork. Transfer to a platter and cover to retain heat.

In a medium saucepot, heat ½ cup olive oil over moderately low heat, add garlic and crushed red pepper. Cook 1 minute or until fragrant. Stir in anchovy paste. Toss in tomatoes, olives, and capers. Add 1/3 c parsley and stir to combine for 2 minutes. Reduce heat and simmer for 5 minutes.

Spoon sauce over roughy, garnish with remaining parsley and pass arounf the table with freshly grated Parmesan cheese and crushed red pepper

Makes 4 to 6 servings

seafood mains

ON THE BACK COVER
CIDER HERB SALMON FILLET OVER BLACK & ORANGE RICE

4 T oil

1 c onion, julienned

1 c butternut squash, peeled, seeded and diced

3 cloves garlic, sliced

3½ c water

2 c black rice

1 t salt

Eight 4 to 5-oz salmon fillets

Pepper

1 c apple cider or apple juice

1 c vegetable stock

½ c dry white wine

2 T cornstarch

2 T apple cider vinegar

1 t dried sage

Pecans, toasted and chopped

Black rice is a premium medium-grain rice that was once the exclusive grain of Chinese emperors. When cooked, it is not sticky like other rice. It has a nutty flavor and turns rich purple.

Preheat oven to 350°F. Line a sheet pan with parchment paper.

In a medium saucepan, heat 1 tablespoon oil over medium heat. Add onion, squash, and garlic. Cook 5 minutes or until tender. Remove from saucepan. Add water, rice, and salt to the saucepan. Bring to a boil. Reduce heat, cover and simmer 30 minutes or until rice is tender and water is absorbed. Fold in cooked vegetables.

Meanwhile in a large skillet, heat remaining 3 tablespoons oil over high heat. Season salmon with salt and pepper. Place salmon in skillet, presentation side down. Sear until just browned. Transfer to prepared pan. Bake 8 to 10 minutes until fish just flakes when tested with a fork.

In the same skillet, combine apple cider, vegetable stock, and wine. Bring to a boil, stirring with a wooden spoon to scrape up any browned bits from the bottom of the skillet. Whisk together cornstarch and vinegar and add to skillet gradually, whisking continuously until thickened and bubbly. Add sage and season to taste with salt and pepper.

Serve salmon with rice, lightly cover with cider herb sauce and top with toasted pecans.

Makes 8 servings

SHRIMP AND CRISPY BACON OVER CHEESY GRITS

2 c skim milk

2 c water

1 t salt

1 c yellow cornmeal grits

1 c white cheddar cheese, shredded

3 T butter

1 T oil

4 slices slab bacon, chopped, crisp-cooked, reserve rendered fat

1½ lbs medium shrimp, peeled and deveined

1½ c onion, chopped

3 cloves garlic, minced

3 T cornstarch

1½ c chicken broth

1 c heavy cream

1 t cayenne pepper

1 t hot sauce

½ t each salt and pepper

½ c scallion, chopped

¼ c fresh Italian flat leaf parsley, chopped

Absolutely delish! I created for World Food & Wine Fest.

In a large pot over medium heat, add the milk, water and salt. Bring to a simmer. Whisk in the grits. Continue to whisk briskly until they begin to thicken to help eliminate lumps. Cook the grits for 10 to 15 minutes, stirring occasionally, until completely thickened. Stir in cheese and 2 tablespoons of butter. Cover and set aside.

In a large skillet, heat oil over medium heat in the same pan as the rendered bacon fat. Add the shrimp and cook for 1 to 2 minutes on each side until they turn pale. Transfer the shrimp to a platter and keep warm.

Add the onions to the skillet and cook 5 minutes until softened. Stir in the garlic and cook for 1 minute. Sprinkle in the cornstarch and cook for an additional minute. Whisk in the chicken stock and cook until the sauce begins to thicken. Whisk in the cream, remaining tablespoon of butter, cayenne pepper, hot sauce, salt, and pepper. Continue cooking until the sauce starts to thicken more. Return the shrimp to the pan and cook for 3 to 4 minutes, making sure not to overcook the shrimp.

Serve shrimp sauce over grits in a shallow bowl. Garnish with the bacon, green onions, and parsley.

Makes 6 generous servings

seafood mains

GRILLED HALIBUT

2 T olive oil

1 T lime juice

½ t salt

½ t ground cumin

¼ t cayenne pepper

Four to six 5-oz halibut or other firm fish steaks, cut ¾ to 1-inch thick

1 recipe Peach Salsa (page 144)

OR

1 recipe Chili Garlic Sauce (page 143)

Preheat an outdoor grill with a high heat zone and a low heat zone.

In a small bowl, combine oil, lime juice, salt, cumin, and cayenne pepper. Spread mixture on presentation side of fish steaks.

Place fish steaks on a greased grill rack directly over high heat. Cover and grill 3 to 5 minutes to brown on one side. Rotate a quarter turn and grill same amount of time to brown. Flip over and repeat browning process. Move fish to low side and cook until 150°F.

Serve on platter with Peach Salsa or Chili Garlic Sauce.

Makes 4 to 6 servings

I don't care about my own life. The most important thing is that I complete my mission, the work that the Lord Jesus gave me – to tell people the Good News about God's grace.

ACTS 20:24

When you invite people into your home for dinner and they offer to help, let them! People always want to help.

sauces & spreads

24 HOLLANDAISE SAUCE

25 SPINACH PESTO

26 CHAMPAGNE MUSTARD CREAM SAUCE

27 WHISKEY BUTTER

27 APPLE SAGE STUFFING

29 APPLE WALNUT BACON STUFFING

29 CIDER SAUCE

25 WHISKEY PEPPER CREAM SAUCE

29 TOMATILLO SAUCE

26 POBLANO PESTO

28 PEANUT SAUCE

28 CHILI GARLIC SAUCE

29 PEACH SALSA

29 LEMON MORNAY SAUCE

HOLLANDAISE SAUCE

3 egg yolks

½ t Dijon mustard

½ t lemon zest

Pinch cayenne pepper

½ cup (1 stick) butter, melted and hot to cook the egg yolks

Salt and pepper

My blender Hollandaise is so easy and delicious. Pour over Beef Tenderloin Eggs Benedict (page 18) or plain poached eggs and use any leftover drizzled over asparagus.

In a blender combine egg yolks, Dijon, lemon zest, and cayenne until smooth. While blender is running, add butter in a thin stream through the opening in the lid until incorporated. Add salt and pepper to taste.

If it's too thick add a small amount of hot water.

SPINACH PESTO

2 c (9 oz) fresh spinach, washed

1 c (4 oz) hard cheese (Parmesan, Asiago or Manchego) in chunks

⅓ c packed fresh basil

½ c pine nuts, toasted

2 cloves garlic

½ c olive oil

Salt and pepper

This pesto is so wonderfully versatile! Use on Italian "Love Apple" Soup (page 56), Spaghetti Squash (page 74), or Baked Salmon (page 122).

In a food processor, combine spinach, cheese, basil, pine nuts, and garlic. Pulse until chopped, scraping down sides.

With processor running, drizzle in olive oil.

Season to taste with salt and pepper.

sauces & spreads

CHAMPAGNE MUSTARD CREAM SAUCE

2 c dry brut Champagne

¼ c diced shallots

2 T Dijon mustard

½ c heavy cream

1 cup (2 sticks) cold unsalted butter, cut into small pieces

½ t salt

½ t white pepper

1½ c green grapes, halved

I wanted something elegant. I can see this for a celebration like an anniversary. I think grapes are underutilized, and I love mustard in a sauce. This is fantastic over chicken breasts!

In a medium saucepan, combine Champagne and shallots. Bring to a boil. Reduce heat to medium low and simmer about 7 minutes or until the mixture is almost reduced. Stir in mustard. Add cream and return to a boil. Cook 3 minutes or until reduced by half. Turn the heat to low and whisk in the butter, 1 tablespoon at a time, adding each piece before the previous one has completely incorporated. Remove the pan from the heat periodically to prevent the sauce from getting too hot and breaking. Continue until all of butter pieces have been added and the sauce coats the back of a spoon. Season the sauce with salt and white pepper. Stir in grapes.

Spoon luscious sauce over chicken.

WHISKEY BUTTER

½ cup (1 stick) butter, softened

1 T chopped fresh parsley

1 T Jack Daniels whiskey

1 t snipped fresh chives

1 t Dijon mustard

1 t Worcestershire sauce

½ t salt

½ t white pepper

Place a dollop of Whiskey Butter onto a pork chop and Oh my!!!

In a small bowl, stir together all ingredients.

Garnish with additional parsley.

APPLE SAGE STUFFING

6 slices bacon, chopped

2 Granny Smith apples, peeled and diced

2 shallots, finely chopped

1 T fresh ginger, minced

1 T fresh sage, chopped

1 c fontina cheese, cubed

This is one option for stuffing inside Iowa Pork Chops (page 98) or anything else you desire!

In a large skillet, fry bacon until crisp. Remove from skillet, drain on paper towels. Reserve 3 tablespoons drippings in the skillet.

Cook apples, shallots, and ginger in hot bacon drippings over medium high for 5 minutes or until tender.

Remove from heat and let cool. Stir in sage, chopped bacon, and cheese.

APPLE WALNUT BACON STUFFING

1 T olive oil

1 T butter

1 Granny Smith apple, peeled, cored and diced

½ c leek, sliced

½ t fresh thyme, chopped

½ t fresh sage, chopped

1 clove garlic, minced

½ c crisp cooked crumbled bacon

⅓ c toasted walnuts, coarsely chopped

¼ c Parmesan cheese, shredded

Another amazing option for stuffing inside Iowa Pork Chops (page 98) or any other type of meat.

Heat a large skillet over medium high heat. Add oil and butter. When hot and melted, add apple, leek, thyme, sage, and garlic. Cook 4 minutes until tender. Transfer to a bowl. Let cool slightly, then stir in bacon, walnuts, and Parmesan.

sauces & spreads

CIDER SAUCE

1½ c apple cider or juice

1 c dry white wine

1 T chicken base (Better Than Bouillon®)

1 T cornstarch

1 T apple cider vinegar

Salt and pepper

This zingy yet sweet sauce is a perfect addition to Stuffed Iowa Pork Chops (page 98) and Cornbread Stuffed Roasted Turkey Breast (page 103). Yum!

Add cider, wine and chicken base to skillet. Bring to a boil over medium high heat, stirring with a wooden spoon to loosen bits from the bottom of the pan.

In a small bowl whisk together cornstarch and vinegar. Drizzle into boiling to sauce, stirring constantly, until thickened and bubbly. Season to taste.

Turn down to low until ready to serve.

WHISKEY PEPPER CREAM SAUCE

3 T butter

1 small red onion, julienned

2 cloves garlic, coarsely chopped

⅓ c all-purpose flour

1 t cracked pepper

1 c beef broth

⅓ c whiskey

2 T capers

¼ c cream

⅓ c chopped fresh parsley

I like to incorporate liquor into dishes. Spoon this sauce over grilled beef tenderloin...Mmm! You won't regret it.

In a large skillet, heat butter over medium heat. Add onion and garlic. Cook and stir 5 minutes until tender. Stir in flour and pepper. Cook 1 minute. Add broth, whiskey, and capers. Bring to a boil. Cook and stir until thickened and bubbly. Stir in cream and parsley. Season to taste with salt and pepper.

TOMATILLO SAUCE

½ lb tomatillos, husks and stems removed

½ c chicken stock

¼ c scallions, cut in 1-inch pieces

1 small to medium jalapeño pepper, seeded and chopped

2 T fresh lime juice

1 to 2 cloves garlic, chopped

½ t sugar

¼ t salt

⅓ c packed fresh cilantro

Tomatillos aren't often talked about. This sauce gives dishes a real southwestern flare. Drizzle overtop grilled chicken seasoned with cumin and garlic. Pairs nicely with hot sauce, too.

In a medium saucepan, combine tomatillos and stock. Bring to a boil over medium high heat. Reduce to a simmer, cover, and cook 8 minutes or until fork tender. Drain.

In food processor, combine tomatillos, scallions, jalapeño, lime juice, garlic, sugar, and salt. Process until smooth. Adjust seasoning with additional salt and pepper. Add cilantro and pulse briefly to chop.

POBLANO PESTO

2 medium poblano chile peppers

½ fresh cilantro, chopped

¼ c (1 oz) Cotija cheese, crumbled

2 T pine nuts, toasted

2 cloves garlic, quarted

¼ t crushed red pepper

Salt and pepper

Olive oil

Serve atop Espresso and Chili Rubbed Flank Steak (page 109) for a surprisingly wonderful combination of flavors!

Cut peppers in half lengthwise; remove stems, seeds, and membranes. Coarsely chop peppers and place in a food processor with cilantro, cheese, pine nuts, garlic, and crushed red pepper. Cover and process until mixture is finely chopped. With processor running, slowly add oil in a steady stream through feed tube to form a coarse paste. Season to taste with salt and pepper.

sauces & spreads

PEANUT SAUCE

1 c chunky peanut butter

¾ c canned unsweetened coconut milk

⅓ c diced onion

2 t minced garlic

½ t fresh ginger, minced

½ t soy sauce

1 t lime juice

Pinch red pepper flakes

Serve with Chicken Satay (page 31) or toss with stir fry!

In a small saucepan, combine all ingredients. Cook over low heat stirring constantly, 10 minutes or until creamy. May need to add water for desired thickness/thinness.

CHILI GARLIC SAUCE

⅔ c water

⅔ c sugar

½ c rice vinegar

4 t cornstarch

2 t garlic, minced

1 t chili garlic paste

1 t soy sauce

2 T cilantro, chopped

This sauce is amazing with seafood! Drizzle over Crisy Sea Scallops (page 123) or Grilled Halibut (page 128), plus use as a dressing on Crispy Cod Market Salad (page 48).

In a medium saucepan, combine water, sugar, vinegar, cornstarch, garlic, paste, and soy sauce. Bring to a boil. Cool slightly then stir in cilantro. Adjust seasoning with additional sugar, chili paste, or salt to taste.

Makes approximately 2 cups

sauces & spreads

PEACH SALSA

1 to 2 (1 c) peaches, peeled or unpeeled, seeded, and chopped

2 (1½ c) medium tomatoes, chopped

1 medium avocado, peeled, coarsely chopped

1 small jalapeño, finely chopped

¼ c fresh cilantro, coarsely chopped

2 (2 T) green onions, thinly sliced

1 clove garlic, finely chopped

2 t lime juice

¼ t salt or to taste

The sky is the limit with this delectable fresh salsa. Serve over Grilled Halibut (page 128) or use as a tapenade on toasted baguette slices. Yum!

In a medium bowl combine all ingredients. It's best at room temperature.

LEMON MORNAY SAUCE

2½ T butter

2 T all-purpose flour

2 c warmed milk

¼ t salt

⅛ t white pepper

2 oz fontina or Swiss cheese, shredded

1 t lemon zest

Fresh parsley, chopped

I use this to top off Stuffed & Baked Tilapia (page 124).

In a medium saucepan, melt butter over medium high heat. Add flour, stirring constantly to cook and until it becomes a pale yellow, about 1 minute. Do not allow to brown. Slowly add the milk, whisking until the sauce thickens and comes to a boil, about 2 to 3 minutes. Reduce to simmer and season with salt and pepper. Stir in the cheese and lemon zest and whisk until melted. If the sauce seems too thick, thin with a little milk.

Like most chefs, I understand I can be an intimidating dinner guest. People will say 'I can't believe I'm having a chef over for dinner.' I love all food. If you make a peanut butter and jelly sandwich, and I make one, yours is going to taste better because you made it for me.

desserts

148   CHEF TERRIE'S FAMOUS FLAMBÉED BANANAS FOSTER WITH ICE CREAM

149   APPLE CRISP

150   CHOCOLATE DIPPED CANNOLI WITH PISTACHIO NUTS

151   CARROT CAKE WITH CREAM CHEESE FROSTING

152   BAILEY'S IRISH CHOCOLATE MOUSSE IN A CHOCOLATE CUP

153   FRIED ICE CREAM

154   GRILLED PEACHES & ANGEL FOOD CAKE WITH TOASTED ALMONDS

155   HOLIDAY PUMPKIN TIRAMISU

156   CARAMEL APPLE BREAD PUDDING WITH BRANDY BUTTER

157   BASIL LIME POUND CAKE

158   GINGERSNAP PUMPKIN CUSTARD BRÛLÉE

159   ITALIAN LEMON CAKE WITH ROSEMARY AND GOLDEN RAISINS

160   LAVENDER SHORTBREAD COOKIES

161   STRAWBERRY MARGARITA TIRAMISU

162   RUSTIC APPLE GALETTE

163   SWEET CORN CRÈME BRÛLÉE

164   LAVENDER LEMONADE

CHEF TERRIE'S FAMOUS FLAMBÉED BANANAS FOSTER WITH ICE CREAM

¾ cup (1½ sticks) butter

1¼ c brown sugar, packed

6 firm bananas, peeled and sliced thick

⅓ c 151 Rum

Blue Bunny Premium Vanilla Bean Ice Cream

This iconic dessert was created at New Orleans' Brennan's Restaurant in the 1950s. It was named for Richard Foster, a regular Brennan's customer.

People love to watch foods flambéed. I always turn the lights down low and say "Oopah!" It's the most decadent dessert you can imagine, and much simpler than it looks! I strongly recommend Blue Bunny Premium Vanilla Bean ice cream.

Even though it's called "Bananas Foster," use your imagination – try peaches and cinnamon or pineapple with coconut sorbet.

Pre-scoop medium to large ice cream balls and freeze onto a parchment lined baking sheet.

In a large skillet, melt the butter over medium low heat. Add the brown sugar and stir until completely dissolved, about 2 minutes. Add the bananas to the pan and cook until they become slightly soft and come to a boil. Remove the pan from the heat and add the rum.

Carefully ignite the alcohol with a long kitchen lighter to flambé. Wait until flames die out to serve. Place a lid overtop to extinguish the flames if necessary.

Divide the ice cream among dessert bowls and spoon delectable sauce with bananas overtop.

Makes 6 to 8 servings

APPLE CRISP

½ c all-purpose flour

⅔ c packed brown sugar

⅔ c rolled oats

½ cup (1 stick) cold butter

10 Granny Smith apples, peeled, cored, and thinly sliced

1 c granulated sugar

3 T cornstarch

¾ t ground cinnamon

¼ t ground nutmeg, fresh is best

¼ t salt

Preheat oven to 375°F.

For topping, combine flour, brown sugar, and oats. Using your hands or a pastry blender, cut in butter until mixture resembles coarse crumbs.

For filling, toss together apples, sugar, cornstarch, spices, and salt. Pour into 13x9 baking dish. Crumble topping over filling.

Bake 40 to 50 minutes or until crumb topping is golden brown and apples are tender.

Serve with ice cream or whipped cream.

Makes 10 to 12 servings

CHOCOLATE DIPPED CANNOLI WITH PISTACHIO NUTS

¾ c chocolate chips

8 large cannoli shells, purchased from an Italian market or generally found in the grocery pasta section

2 c ricotta cheese

3 T sugar

1 T orange zest

1½ t vanilla

¾ c mini semi-sweet chocolate chips

½ c pistachio nuts, chopped

In a 2-cup glass measuring cup, microwave ¾ cup chocolate chips, stirring every 20 seconds until melted.

Dip one end of cannoli shell to cover edges in chocolate and place on parchment paper. Refrigerate while making filling to firm the chocolate.

In a medium bowl, whisk together cheese, sugar, zest, and vanilla. Add mini chocolate chips.

Scoop into piping bag and squeeze into shells so the ricotta mixture is emerging from the ends slightly.

Dip one end of the cannoli into chopped pistachio nuts to coat the filling. Refrigerate until ready to serve, but not too long or shell will become soft.

Makes 8 servings

CARROT CAKE WITH CREAM CHEESE FROSTING

3 c all-purpose flour

2 c granulated sugar

1 t baking soda

1 t ground cinnamon

½ t salt

2 c shredded carrots, no need to peel

1⅓ c vegetable oil

2 eggs, lightly beaten

One 15-oz can crushed pineapple, drained

1 c toasted chopped pecans

¾ c raisins

FROSTING

8 oz cream cheese, softened

2 T warm water

2 t clear vanilla

6 c sifted powdered sugar

Preheat oven to 350°F. Grease two 8-inch round cake pans and line bottoms with parchment paper.

In a large bowl, combine flour, sugar, baking soda, cinnamon, and salt. Add carrots, vegetable oil, and eggs. Beat with an electric mixer on medium speed until well mixed. Stir in pineapple, pecans, and raisins. Pour batter into prepared pans and bake for 25 minutes or until moist crumbs stick to toothpick. Cool in pans on wire rack for 10 minutes. Remove from pans and cool completely on wire racks.

For the frosting, beat cream cheese with an electric mixer on medium speed for 30 seconds. Beat in water and vanilla until combined. Gradually add sugar and beat until smooth.

Frosting recipe will cover the tops of two cake layers thickly or the entire cake in a thin layer. I like a lot of frosting and double the recipe to cover cakes. I also like to sprinkle additional chopped toasted nuts on top or around the side.

desserts

BAILEY'S IRISH CHOCOLATE MOUSSE IN A CHOCOLATE CUP

12 oz chocolate

6 to 8 balloons, blown up baseball size

MOUSSE

½ c unsweetened cocoa powder

1 t instant coffee crystals

Pinch salt

2 c heavy whipping cream

⅔ c powdered sugar

¼ c Bailey's Irish Cream

Melt chocolate over double boiler or microwave. If using a double boiler, bring water to a boil in a small saucepan. Add a double boiler insert or a heatproof bowl to the top of the saucepan. Reduce heat to medium low. Add chocolate to the double boiler insert or bowl, stirring until melted. If using microwave, place chocolate in a medium microwave-safe bowl. Microwave for 1 to 2 minutes, stirring every 30 seconds or until melted. Watch closely.

Let chocolate cool slightly and dip balloons halfway into bowl. Coat heavily, 1/8-inch thick. May dip multiple times.

Set up on parchment paper on a baking sheet or tray and place in freezer for 10 minutes.

Snip hole in balloon to deflate and carefully remove balloon from inside chocolate cups.

For mousse, whisk cocoa powder, coffee, and salt together in a small bowl. Set aside.

Whip the cream for 1 minute on medium high, then add powdered sugar. Whip 1 minute more or until stiff peaks form. Add Bailey's and coffee mixture. Whip on high one more minute for stiff peaks.

Pipe equally into prepared chocolate cups.

Makes 6 to 8 servings

"FRIED" ICE CREAM

2 c vanilla ice cream, or a favorite flavor

1½ c Honey Bunches of Oats® cereal

3 T honey

¼ t ground cinnamon

Whipped Cream

Stemmed Maraschino cherries

This is a healthier version of a traditional Mexican fried ice cream. I drizzle mine with chocolate and caramel. Yummy!

Pre-scoop 4 to 6 ice cream balls. Place in freezer on a parchment-lined baking sheet until firm, about 2 hours.

Place cereal in zip-top bag and crush into crumbs using a meat mallet or rolling pin. Transfer to a bowl and roll each ice cream ball in the crumbs then return them to the freezer for at least another hour or until firm.

When ready to serve, combine honey and cinnamon in a small bowl warm in microwave 30 to 45 seconds to thin, or heat in saucepan on low.

Place ice cream ball in serving bowl, drizzle with honey, and top with whipped cream and a cherry. Serve immediately.

Makes 4 to 6 servings

GRILLED PEACHES & ANGEL FOOD CAKE WITH TOASTED ALMONDS

¾ c sliced almonds

1½ c whipping cream

½ c (1 stick) butter, melted

2 t sugar

1 t ground cinnamon

7 medium peaches, halved and pitted

1 ready-made or scratch angel food cake, sliced

Fresh mint

Preheat an outdoor grill to medium high heat.

Preheat oven to 350°F. Place almonds on a baking sheet. Bake 8 to 10 minutes or until fragrant.

In a medium bowl, whip cream, increasing speed gradually until soft peaks form.

In a small bowl, combine butter, sugar, and cinnamon. Brush over peaches. Place peaches, cut side down, on a greased grill rack directly over heat. Cover and grill 5 minutes until golden grill marks form. Turn and grill 3 minutes on the other side. Slice peaches.

Add angel food cake slices to the grill. Grill briefly on both sides for golden grill marks and grilled flavor.

On each serving plate, place a slice of cake, peaches, and a mound of whipped cream. Garnish with mint and additional cinnamon if desired.

Makes 8 servings

HOLIDAY PUMPKIN TIRAMISU

15-oz can pumpkin

8-oz package cream cheese, softened

½ c powdered sugar

¼ c crystallized ginger, chopped

1½ t vanilla

¾ t ground cinnamon

¼ t ground nutmeg

Two 3-oz packages ladyfingers

Sweetened whipped cream

Freshly grated nutmeg

Fresh mint sprigs and/or gingersnaps

In a food processor, combine pumpkin, cream cheese, sugar, ginger, vanilla, cinnamon, and nutmeg. Pulse until combined. Transfer mixture to a piping bag.

Line inside of a pretty bowl, individual café cup, wine glass, or ramekin with ladyfingers. Pipe in pumpkin mousse, then lay another layer of ladyfingers, then mousse again. Refrigerate 2 hours to set up.

To serve, dollop whipped cream on top, sprinkle with fresh grated nutmeg, and garnish with mint and/or ginger snaps.

Makes 6 to 8 servings

CARAMEL APPLE BREAD PUDDING WITH BRANDY BUTTER

8 eggs, lightly beaten

1 c granulated sugar

4 c milk

¼ t salt

½ loaf Texas toast bread, exclude heels, remove crust and cut into 1-inch cubes

¾ c toasted walnuts, chopped

¾ c Granny Smith apple, peeled and diced

¾ c caramel chips or caramel apple dip

BRANDY BUTTER

½ c (1 stick) unsalted butter, softened

1 c powdered sugar

1½ t brandy

1½ t vanilla

Preheat oven to 325°F. Grease a 9x13-inch baking dish.

In a large bowl, beat together eggs and sugar until combined. Beat in milk and salt until combined. Add bread and stir to coat. Pour into a prepared dish. Sprinkle nuts, apples, and caramel chips over the mixture.

Bake for 45 to 60 minutes or until center is cooked through. A knife inserted in the center should come out clean.

For Brandy Butter, beat together butter and sugar until light and fluffy. Add brandy and vanilla. Beat until incorporated.

Serve warm with a dollop of Brandy Butter on top of each serving. It will melt into a sauce.

Makes 8 to 10 servings

BASIL LIME POUND CAKE

1 c sour cream

½ t baking soda

1 c packed fresh basil leaves

1 c granulated sugar, plus a little to prepare the pan

1 c powdered sugar

1 c butter, at room temperature

2 large eggs

1 T lime zest

1 t vanilla

½ t salt

2½ c all-purpose flour

Whipped cream

Preheat oven to 350°F. Grease a 10-inch Bundt® pan and sprinkle with sugar.

In a small bowl, mix sour cream with baking soda. Set aside.

In a food processor, process basil and sugars. Add butter, eggs, zest, vanilla, and salt. Process until smooth. Add soda and sour cream mixture. Pulse to combine. Add flour and pulse only until the flour is well-mixed. Careful not to over-process.

Place batter in pan and bake 1 hour or until a tester stick comes out with moist crumbs.

Cool 10 minutes on a wire rack, then invert cake onto a large platter.

Fill or serve with fresh whipped cream

Makes 10 to 12 servings

GINGERSNAP PUMPKIN CUSTARD BRÛLÉE

1 c crushed gingersnaps

3 T butter, melted and cooled

2 T brown sugar

3 large eggs

½ c sugar, plus extra for caramelizing

1¾ c heavy whipping cream

1 c canned pumpkin purée

½ t ground cinnamon

½ t ground nutmeg

1 pinch ground ginger

1 pinch ground cloves

Preheat oven to 325°F.

In a small bowl, combine gingersnaps, butter, and brown sugar. Press into bottoms of eight 4-oz ramekins.

In a medium bowl, whisk together eggs and sugar until well blended.

In a medium saucepan, heat heavy whipping cream, almost to a simmer, stirring frequently to prevent scorching.

Slowly add hot cream to egg mixture while whisking. (Adding it too quickly can result in scrambled eggs.) Whisk in pumpkin purée and spices.

Divide the mixture into ramekins and place in a large casserole baking dish, or into two dishes. Fill the baking dish with boiling water about halfway up the sides of the ramekins. Bake for 35 to 40 minutes or until centers barely wiggle when you move the pan. Transfer from baking dish(es) to a wire rack. Cool to room temperature then cover and refrigerate for at least 4 hours.

When ready to serve, caramelize either using a culinary blowtorch or broiler.

If using a torch, sprinkle custards with 1 to 2 teaspoons sugar, then heat, moving in a circular pattern until the whole surface is caramelized and sugar turns a rich amber color.

If broiling, place ramekins on a baking sheet and let stand at room temperature for 15 minutes. Sprinkle with sugar. Broil 8 inches from the heat for 4 to 7 minutes or until sugar is caramelized.

Makes 8 servings

Notes: Don't caramelize until ready to serve. Don't refrigerate after caramelizing or the sugar will melt.

ITALIAN LEMON CAKE WITH ROSEMARY AND GOLDEN RAISINS

Nonstick cooking spray

1 c all-purpose flour

1 t dried rosemary, crushed

1 t baking powder

¼ t baking soda

⅛ t salt

½ c sugar

3 T olive oil

⅓ c plain fat-free yogurt or sour cream

1 large egg

1 large egg white

1 t vanilla

¼ c golden raisins, currants, dried cranberries or dried blueberries

2 t lemon zest

Sweetened whipped cream

GLAZE

¼ c sugar

¼ c water

1 t lemon zest

2 T lemon juice

Preheat oven to 350°F. Coat a 9-inch round cake pan with nonstick spray.

In a medium bowl, combine flour, rosemary, baking powder, baking soda, and salt.

In a large bowl, combine sugar and olive oil. Beat with an electric mixer on high for 2 minutes. Add yogurt/sour cream, egg, egg white, and vanilla, beating an additional minute. Add flour mixture and beat on low until well blended. Fold in raisins and zest. Pour batter into prepared pan. Bake for 25 minutes or until a toothpick comes out with moist crumbs. Pierce cake lightly with a fork several times.

Combine glaze ingredients, stirring until sugar dissolves.

Spoon glaze over top, a little at a time, allowing to spill down sides.

Cut and serve with fresh whipped cream.

Makes 8 servings

LAVENDER SHORTBREAD COOKIES

1 c granulated sugar

1 T dried culinary lavender buds

2½ c all-purpose flour

½ c cornstarch

¼ t salt

1½ c (3 sticks) butter, softened

¼ c powdered sugar, sifted

1 t lemon zest

Lavender food coloring

In a food processor, combine 2/3 cup granulated sugar and lavender. Pulse until lavender is pulverized.

In a medium bowl, combine flour, cornstarch, and salt. Set aside.

In a large bowl, beat butter, lavender sugar, and powdered sugar with an electric mixer until light and fluffy. Add zest and flour mixture and mix well.

Divide dough into two 1½-inch diameter cylinders.

In a small bowl, tint remaining 1/3 cup granulated sugar with lavender food coloring.

Roll dough cylinders in tinted sugar and wrap in plastic wrap. Refrigerate 1 hour or until firm.

Preheat the oven to 325°F. Slice dough into ¼ inch cookies. Place on parchment-lined cookie sheets.

Bake for 8 to 10 minutes, just until cookies begin to brown at the edges. Cool for a few minutes on the baking sheets then transfer to wire racks to cool completely.

STRAWBERRY MARGARITA TIRAMISU

Two 8-oz packages cream cheese, softened

½ c powdered sugar

2 T tequila

2 T triple sec

Zest of 2 limes

1 c strawberries, quartered

Two 3-oz packages ladyfingers

1 c strawberries, diced

1 T granulated sugar

Fresh mint

For filling, in a food processor, combine cream cheese, sugar, alcohol, and lime zest. Pulse until smooth. Add 1 cup quartered strawberries and pulse to coarsely chop.

Place a small dab of filling in the bottom of a margarita glass. Lay 3 ladyfingers side-by-side over the filling. Spread a layer of filling over ladyfingers. Lay 3 ladyfingers side-by-side in the opposite direction. Repeat with another layer of filling. Refrigerate until ready to serve.

In a small bowl, combine 1 cup diced strawberries and granulated sugar.

To serve, garnish with a spoonful of the strawberry sugar topping and fresh mint. Very pretty!

Makes 8 servings

desserts

RUSTIC APPLE GALETTE

4 Granny Smith apples, peeled, cored and diced (or equivalent amount of pears, peaches, grapes, or other fruit)

⅓ c walnuts, chopped and toasted (or other nut)

⅓ c raisins, golden raisins, or currants (or other dried fruit)

1½ t ground cinnamon

½ t ground nutmeg

17.3-oz package of Pepperidge Farm® puff pastry sheets, cut each into 4x4 squares for 8 total

4 T butter

Milk

Raw sugar or turbinado sugar

You can combine any combination of spices, fruits, and nuts to make these uniquely your own!

Preheat oven to 375°F. Line a baking sheet with parchment paper.

Combine fruit, nuts, dried fruit, cinnamon, and nutmeg. Place equal amounts of the mixture in the center of each puff pastry square. Gather up accordion style – pleating the sides, and leave the top open. Place ½ T butter on top of each. Brush with milk and sprinkle with sugar. Place on prepared baking sheet. Bake 20 minutes or until golden brown.

Serve with vanilla bean or cinnamon ice cream.

Makes 8 servings

SWEET CORN CRÈME BRÛLÉE

1½ c fresh or frozen corn, thawed

3½ T butter

3 c heavy whipping cream

1 c milk

8 egg yolks

1¼ c plus 2 T sugar, divided

2 T vanilla

Preheat oven to 325°F.

In a large saucepan, cook corn in butter over medium high heat for 30 minutes or until tender. Reduce heat. Add cream and milk. Heat until bubbles form around sides of pan. Cool slightly. Transfer to a blender, or use an immersion blender, to process until smooth. Strain and discard corn pulp. Return to pan.

In a small bowl, whisk together egg yolks and 1¼ cup sugar. Temper by stirring a small amount of hot cream into egg mixture. Pour into the pan, stirring constantly. Stir in vanilla.

Transfer to six 6-oz ramekins. Place in a baking pan. Add 1 inch of boiling water to pan. Bake, uncovered, 40 to 45 minutes or until centers are just set. Mixture will jiggle. Remove ramekins from water bath and cool for 10 minutes on a wire rack. Cover and refrigerate for at least 4 hours.

When ready to serve, caramelize either using a culinary blowtorch or broiler.

If using a torch, sprinkle custards with remaining sugar, then heat, moving in a circular pattern until the whole surface is caramelized and sugar turns a rich amber color.

If broiling, place ramekins on a baking sheet and let stand at room temperature for 15 minutes. Sprinkle with sugar. Broil 8 inches from the heat for 4 to 7 minutes or until sugar is caramelized.

Makes 6 servings

Notes: Don't caramelize until ready to serve. Don't refrigerate after caramelizing or the sugar will melt.

desserts

LAVENDER LEMONADE

1 c lemon juice

1 c sugar

1 T (heaping) dried culinary lavender

6½ c water

When using lavender in cooking, make sure you get a culinary lavender. You can get it at Whole Foods or a spice shop. This refreshing drink is perfect for a summer tea or a bridal or baby shower.

In a small saucepan, combine lemon juice, sugar, and lavender. Bring to boil. Remove from heat. Let cool and strain.

In a pitcher, add infused lavender simple syrup to water and chill.

May your day begin and end with a peaceful sense of the Lord's presence, a quiet heart, and a thankful spirit.

Me and Mom

Every spring, as reliably as the flowers that came up in the yard, Mom would serve daffodil cake to her bridge club. She was very protective of that recipe. I asked her permission to use it in this book (and I got it! See page 186.). Daffodil cake is an angel food cake divided into a yellow part and a white part. The yellow part gets its color from egg yolk and lemon.

mom's recipe collection

- *168* MOSTACCIOLI NOODLE SALAD
- *169* SAUERKRAUT SALAD
- *170* STUFFED CABBAGE ROLLS
- *171* 3 BEAN SALAD
- *172* SUKIYAKI
- *173* 5 DECKER DINNER
- *174* BEEF INTERNATIONAL
- *175* BOK CHOY (BEEF & PEA PODS)
- *176* CHICKEN DELIGHT CASSEROLE
- *177-179* CHOW HAR LOCK/ SWEET & SOUR CHICKEN
- *180* CLAM LINGUINE
- *181* CLAM-MUSHROOM LINGUINE
- *182* ORIENTAL PEPPER STEAK
- *183* PRIME RIB
- *184* STIR FRIED BEEF & PEPPER STEAK
- *185* SUMMER SLUSH
- *186* DAFFODIL CAKE, RHUBARB PIE
- *187* SOCK IT TO ME CAKE
- *188* ARMSTRONG GERMAN CHOCOLATE PIE
- *189* RED VELVET CUPCAKES
- *190* RED WALDORF CAKE
- *191* POPCORN BALLS, PECAN PIE
- *192* MONKEY BREAD

Mastaccioli Noodle Salad

- 1 box noodles
- 3/4 c oil
- 3/4 c vinegar
- 3/4 c sugar
- salt
- pepper
- 1/2 t garlic salt
- 1/2 t parsley
- 1 sliced cucumber
- 1 " onion
- green pepper
- tomato

over

Cook noodles, drain & rinse. Add cucumbers & onion.
(Dressing)
Mix remaining ingredients. Pour over noodles. Chill.

Sauerkraut Salad

Drain 2 c sauerkraut.
Heat ½ c salad oil
⅓ c vinegar + 1 c sugar
Do not cook — Heat til hot
Pour over
  1 c chopped celery
  1 diced green pepper
  ½ c chopped onion
  and sauerkraut
Better made the day before

Stuffed Cabbage Rolls

Place cabbage leaves in large kettle of boiling water, let stand 5 minutes or till limp. Combine 1½ lbs ground beef, 3 C bread crumbs, 1 egg, garlic, 1 t salt, ¼ t pepper, & ¼ t oregano. Spoon about ½ c mixture on each leaf. Roll up. Place in casserole. Combine tomato (1 can) sauce and ½ water, pour over cabbage rolls. Bake 350° 1½ hours.

3 Bean Salad or Mother's Bean Salad

1 can green beans
1 can yellow beans
1 can Kidney beans
1 small jar of Pimento - diced
1 green pepper diced 1 half onion (sliced)
½ cup Oil
½ cup Vinegar
½ cup Sugar
1 Tablespoon Celery Seed or salt
1 Tablespoon Onion Flakes

(over)

Mix all together and refrigerate over night before serving. Salad will keep

Here's what's cookin' Sukiyaki

Recipe from: _____ **Serves:** 6

2 T oil, 1 lb sirloin tip, cut into strips
1 lg onion cut into chunks
3 stalks celery, sliced thick
fresh mushrooms sliced
1 can water chestnuts sliced
1 can bamboo shoots, drained
½ C hot water with 1 ts instant beef bouillon
1 T sugar, 3 T soy sauce
1 T cornstarch

Heat oil in lg skillet. Brown meat quickly, push to one side. Add onion, celery, mushrooms & cook 3 min, stirring constantly. Add water chestnuts, bamboo shoots, bouillon + water. Mix sugar, soy sauce + cornstarch together, stir into mixture. Bring to boil. Cook 2 min. Serve over rice.

5 Decker Dinner

Lay 4 strips of bacon (cut up) on bottom of casserole.

Place hamburger patties on top of bacon.

Then a layer of sliced onions
" " " potatoes
" " " carrots

sprinkle with parsley, salt & pepper

Place on top of stove uncovered until bacon sizzles. Then add 1/4 c water, cover, put in oven, cook 1 hour, can be cooked on top of stove. 350°

Beef Steak Internationale

2 lbs round stk cut in 1/2 by 3 in strips
1 Tbsp shortening
1/2 c mushroom liquid + water
2 med gr peppers in strips
2 onions, sliced thin
1 can cr of celery soup   Salt & pepper
1/2 cup mayonnaise
1 - 3 oz can button mushrooms

Preheat fry pan 375°. Brown meat well, add mushroom liquid, gr peppers & onions. Reduce heat 212°. Cover & cook 25 to 30 min, or until meat is tender. Combine soup, mayonnaise, mushrooms, salt & pepper. Pour over meat mixture & blend well. Cover & heat 20 to 25 min.
Serve over rice.

Bok Choy (Beef & Pea Pods)

Bok Choy — Mushrooms
Pea Pods — Water chestnuts
Bean Sprouts — Bamboo shoots

Slice Bok Choy thin at an angle
Slice chestnuts. Sugar (½ t serving)
Salt   Water Chicken bouillon
Oil
Cornstarch Onion

Cover pan with oil. Brown meat in oil. Add soy sauce.

Cook all veg. including onion until tender. Add bouillon sugar & salt. Simmer, add cornstarch then add meat. Heat through. Serve over rice

13 x 9 pan - grease — 8 servings

Chicken Delight Casserole

6 slices white bread
6 T mayonnaise
1½ lbs cooked chicken cut ½" cubes
   (about 4 cups)
½ lb fresh mushrooms, sliced or canned
2 T oleo
1 can (8½ oz) water chestnuts, sliced (drained)
1 pkg. (8 oz) sharp American cheese slices
1 C milk
4 eggs
1 can cream of mushroom soup
1 can cream of celery soup
¼ t salt, ½ t celery salt
1 jar (2 oz) sliced pimiento (drained)

Spread each slice of bread with mayonnaise, lay in pan, cover with chicken. Cook mushrooms & chestnuts in butter, sprinkle over chicken. Cut cheese slices diagonally in half, arrange in 2 rows (points overlapping). Mix milk, eggs, soups, seasoning & pimiento & pour over casserole. Cover, refrigerate at least 6 hrs no longer than 24 hrs. 350° 1 hr. (can freeze)

Chow Har lock

16-20 shrimp   ½ t salt
1 T flour   2 c oil for deep frying

Batter – 6 T flour   3 T corn starch
½ t salt   pepper   6 T water
1 t baking pwd.   ¼ t soda

Sauce – ¼ ketchup   ½ C sugar
½ C vinegar   1 C water
2 T corn starch dissolved in water
½ green pepper cut in chunks   ½ tomato

Sprinkle salt & flour over shrimp
Batter – mix flour, cornstarch, salt & pepper
add water, then baking pwd & soda
Beat well.
Sauce – place flour ingredients in a
saucepan. Bring to boil – thicken
add gr. pepper & tomato. Bring to
boil again. Remove from heat &
set aside. Heat oil. Dip shrimp
in batter one at a time. Drop a few
shrimp into oil. Deep fry   Serve with
Drain on paper towels   rice

(Chow Har Lock)   Pork or Shrimp

Here's what's cookin' Sweet & Sour Chicken   **Serves** 6
Recipe from the kitchen of _____

2 whole chicken breasts (I use 4) cut up
½ t salt 1 egg beaten
¾ c biscuit mix 1 C oil
⅔ c sugar 2 T cornstarch
1 T paprika 1 (1lb 4oz) can
pineapple chunks ¼ C soy sauce
¼ C vinegar 1 C gr pepper strips
½ c sliced onion
2 medium tomatoes cut up
Hot cooked rice

Sprinkle chicken with salt & coat with egg then biscuit mix. Fry chicken in hot oil (400°) until brown. Remove drain on paper towels. Place in oven to keep warm.
    Combine sugar cornstarch & paprika in 10" skillet. Drain pineapple and enough water to make 2c. Add juice soy sauce + vinegar to cornstarch mixture. Cook stirring constantly until mixture boils. Boil 1 min. Add gr pepper + onion cover cook until tender crisp. Add pineapple tomatoes. heat well add chicken chunks. Serve over rice.

Here's what's cookin': **Sweet & Sour Chicken**
Recipe from: Dan   Serves: 6

4 whole chicken breasts, skinned, boned & cut into 1" chunks
½ t salt, 1 egg beaten
⅓ c biscuit mix, 1 c oil
⅔ c sugar, 2 T cornstarch
1 T paprika, 1 (1 lb 4 oz) can pineapple chunks
¼ c soy sauce, ¼ c cider vinegar
1 c gr pepper strips
½ c sliced onion
2 med tomatoes, cut up
Hot cooked rice

Sprinkle chicken with salt & coat with egg, then biscuit mix. Fry in oil in small skillet until brown. Drain on paper towel. Place in 250° oven to keep warm. Combine sugar & cornstarch & paprika in 10" skillet or dutch oven. Drain pineapple, add enough water to juice to make 2 c. Add juice, soy sauce, vinegar to cornstarch mix. Cook stirring constantly until boil. Boil 1 min. add gr pepper & onion & cover. Simmer 5 min. Do not over cook. Add pineapple & tomatoes. Heat well. Add chicken. Serve over rice.
May use pork or shrimp.

Clam Linguini

1 (6-5) can chopped clams
   drained (keep liquid)
2 cloves garlic chopped
1/4 c olive oil
1 bottle of clam juice
1 T chopped parsley
1/4 t basil leaves
dash pepper

Cook garlic in oil add clam juice + all other ingredients

Bring to boil reduce heat & simmer 5 min, add clams heat thoroughly
Serve over hot linguine

Clam-Mushroom Linguini

- 2 T butter
- 1/4 c green onions
- 1 t chopped garlic
- 1 T flour
- 1 t dijon mustard
- 1 can clams plus juice
- 1 T parsley
- 1 T Basil
- 1/4 t salt
- 1 c sliced mushrooms
- 1/2 c Half & Half
- more liquid if necessary
- Hot cooked linguini - use pasta juice

Melt butter in stir fry pan add onions garlic + mushrooms cook 3 min. Stir in flour + mustard. Add liquid from clams juice Half & Half + pasta water to thick sauce add Herbs + salt Simmer 5 min stirring occasionally add clams + linguini

can use popcorn shrimp

Here's what's cooking: Oriental Pepper Steak

Recipe from the kitchen of:

Sirloin tip - cut in strips
Brown in 2 T hot oil
Add - 1 C bouillon, 1/2 c wine (dry white) 1/3 c soy sauce
2 t sugar, 1/2 t garlic salt
1/2 t ginger, onion cut in lg. chunks, fresh mushrooms, sliced.
Cook 5 min.
Add 1 can bamboo shoots, 1 can water chestnuts, (sliced) and frozen pea pods (1/2 pkg)
Bring to boiling cook 2-3 min or till pea pods are crisp tender.

Mix 1/2 c water + 2 T cornstarch stir into mixture.

Cook till thickened + bubbly.

Serve over rice

6 servings

Prime Rib — 375°

6-8 lb roast
½-1 t. cracked Blk pepper
rub on outside
Place rib side down
on rack in a pan.
Bake 1 hr. Turn oven off
Do not open oven
Remain in oven 3-5 hrs.
Turn oven on again 375°
30-45 min Bake
Do not open oven door
at any time.
Let stand 15 min before
slicing

Stir fried Beef & Pepper Steak *(Can use pea pods & Bamboo shoots)*

3 c cooked rice
1 lb. beef round bottom steak cut into strips
3 T. soy sauce 2 T dry sherry
2 T. cornstarch ¼ t. sugar
⅛ t ground ginger ½ c salad oil
½ lb fresh mushrooms, cut in half
1 medium onion sliced thin, 1 beef bouillon
2 small green & red peppers cut in chunks
½ t salt 1 tomato cut up (Water Chestnuts)

Prepare rice. Cut steak in small thin strips. In small bowl mix soy sauce, sherry, cornstarch, sugar & ginger. Add beef and toss lightly to coat.
In frying pan heat oil till hot. Cook mushrooms, onions, peppers salt and water chestnuts stirring quickly & frequently until tender crisp about 5 min. Spoon vegetables into bowl leaving oil. Add meat to oil, stir fry until meat loses its pink color 2 min. Add veg. and ~~tomato~~ 1 c beef bouillon add tomato. Serve on rice 4 servings

Here's what's cookin' — Summer Slush
Recipe from the kitchen of — Terrie

9 C water   1-12oz frozen lemonade
1½ C sugar   2 C rum
1-12 oz can of frozen orange juice

Boil water & sugar 10 min
add orange juice & lemonade
Stir in Rum. Freeze
To serve mix equal parts
slush & lemon lime (7up)

45 min / 350° — Daffodil Cake - Mom's right one
6 egg whites, 1/2 t cr of tartar, pinch salt
Beat till stiff. Sift 3/4 c sugar +
1/2 c cake flour together + fold
into egg whites. Add 1/2 t vanilla or
almond flavoring.

Yellow part
6 egg yolks 3/4 c sugar pinch salt
Beat 3 minutes
Add 3/4 c flour + 1 tsp baking pwd
to eggs alternately with 1/4 c boiling water.
Add 3/4 t lemon extract. Place
spoonfuls on top of angel mixture

Rhubarb Pie (B-Beck)   350°
2 cups rhubarb
1 cup sugar
3 egg yolks
1 tbsp butter
1 tbsp flour
                  few drops of lemon
Bake in unbaked crust
         about 30 min?
Add meringue after
pie has cooled slightly

Sock It To Me Cake

350
45 min

1 Duncan Hines Butter Cake mix
½ C sugar - ¾ C oil - 1 C sour
cream add 4 eggs one at
a time beating well

Mix together 2 T Brown
sugar + 2 t cinnamon

Pour ½ of batter in Bundt
pan - greased & floured or Pam

Sprinkle sugar & cinnamon
over batter, pour rest of
batter on top

Armstrong German Chocolate Pie

4 oz Bakers German Sweet Choc.
1/4 C butter
1 2/3 C evaporated milk
1 1/2 C sugar
3 T cornstarch
1/8 t salt
2 eggs 1 T vanilla
1 - 10" unbaked pie shell
1 1/3 C coconut
1/2 C pecans

melt choc over low heat add butter, then evaporated milk
In lg bowl mix sugar cornstarch + salt. Beat in eggs + vanilla
Blend in choc
Pour into pie shell.
Sprinkle coconut & pecans on top
Bake 375° 45 min.
Pie sets up as it cools.
chill 4 hrs.

Armstrong's Department Store was "the store" in Cedar Rapids when I was growing up. Mom worked there for 22 years. This recipe is from the in-store restaurant.

Red Velvet Cupcakes

- 2½ c flour
- ½ c cocoa
- 1 t soda
- ½ t salt
- 1 c butter, softened
- 2 c sugar
- 4 eggs
- 1 c sour cream
- ½ c milk
- 2 t vanilla
- 1 - 1 oz Red food coloring

Beat butter + sugar 5 min
Add eggs 1 at a time
Mix in sour cream, milk, red coloring
& vanilla
Beat in flour mixture
Bake 350° 20-25 min.
Frost with cream cheese frosting

- 1 - 8 oz cream cheese
- 4 T soft butter   2 T sour cream
- 2 t vanilla   Beat in 1 box (16 oz) powd sugar

Red Waldorf Cake

350°
30 min

½ c oleo
1½ c sugar
2 eggs
2 oz red food coloring
2 heaping T cocoa
1 c buttermilk
2¼ c flour
1 t vanilla
1 t salt
1 t soda
1 T vinegar

Cream oleo + sugar add eggs. Make paste of food coloring + cocoa add to creamed mixture. Add buttermilk & vanilla alternately with flour mixture. Blend vinegar & soda into mixture.

Popcorn Balls

1 lg Package marshmellows
½ lb. butter
melt together
Pour over at least
4 qts of popped corn — 3 Bags
Let cool first
Form into balls

Jean Eckel's Pecan Pie
1987

3 eggs beaten — 1 cup sugar
1 cup dark syrup — ½ tsp Vinegar
1 tsp Vanilla — 1 tbls melted
Oleo — ¼ tsp salt. 1 cup
pecans. Mix first 5 ingred.
together well, add rest of
the ingred. Put into unbaked
pie shell. Bake at 350° —
40 minutes.

Monkey Bread

4 can biscuits (cut each in 4ths)
roll each piece in
   2/3 c sugar
   1 tsp cinnamon
Let in greased bundt pan
Boil together 2/3 c sugar
          1 stick oleo
          1 tsp vanilla
          1 tsp cinnamon

Pour over biscuits in pan
Bake at 350° - 40 min.
   Turn out on plate.

*The task ahead of me
is never as great
as the power behind me!*

Grandma Hofferber and Mom

My maternal grandmother, Sophie Hofferber, was a pharmacist. She ate healthy, took vitamins, and made well-balanced meals. She was way before her time. She had a huge garden. She canned and pickled. She taught by example. At Grandma Hofferber's, we didn't get casseroles, we got green beans and fruit salads, and her watermelon pickles, from the rind, are emblazoned on my heart.

grandma hofferber's recipes

196 CINNAMON PICKLES

197 WATERMELON PICKLES

198 DATE PINWHEELS

199 SWEET SOUR SPARERIBS

200 HOMEMADE ICE CREAM

201 PUMPKIN PIE

202 BREAD PUDDING

203 OATMEAL BREAD

204 ENGLISH DROP COOKES, OATMEAL COOKIES

205 COFFEE CAKE

RECIPE FOR: Cinnamon pickles
INGREDIENTS: 2 gallon large pickles
rings & sticks
peel - seed.
Cover with water add 1c lime
set 24 hours. Drain & wash
well. Cover with water - let set
3 hours. Drain.

2nd day - 2 qts water, 1C vinegar
1 tsp Alum 1 bottle red food
coloring. Heat this thru & pour
over Cucumber. Soak 3 hours. Wash

~~1C sugar~~
4 sticks cinnamon
2C vinegar
2C water
1 pkg red hots
Heat this until red hots dissolved
Pour over cucumber. Let set 2 days
Then bring all of this to a boil
but do not boil - put in jars
Seal.

Can use green food coloring

PREPARATION TIME: Instead **SERVINGS:**

FROM THE KITCHEN OF: Sophia Hofferber

RECIPE FOR: Watermelon Pickles

INGREDIENTS:

7 lbs prepared rind (peeled & cubed)

2 c vinegar

4 c sugar

½ tsp oil of clove

½ tsp oil of cinnamon

Boil rind until tender but not soft. Drain, bring syrup to boil. Pour over. Let stand overnite. Drain off syrup

DIRECTIONS:

Reheat - pour back over rind do again - 2nd & 3rd day. Heat, put in pint jars & seal
(Heat fruit & syrup)
May add a few maraschino cherries for color.

Date Pinwheels 400°

1 cup Oleo – 1 cup sugar – 1 cup brown sugar – 2 eggs – 1½ tsp Vanilla – 3½ cups flour 1 tsp soda – 1 tsp salt. Mix dough and chill. Divide dough in half, roll out on waxed paper. Fill rolled out dough with date mixture like jelly roll. Slice, bake at 400° for 8 minutes.

Over

2 cups chopped dates
1 cup hot water
⅔ cup sugar – 1 cup chopped nuts
Bring & stir until it boils, then add ⅛ tsp soda. Stir, chill in Refrigerator. Have both items cold. (very good eating)

Sweet Sour Spareribs

3 lb. Spareribs, cut in serving size pieces
2/3 C. Brown sugar firmly packed
2 T. Cornstarch
2 t. dry Mustard
2/3 C. vinegar
1 C. crushed pineapple, undrained
1/2 C. Catsup
1/2 C. water
1/4 C. finely chopped onion
2 T. soy sauce
Salt and Pepper

Spread ribs, meaty side up, in a single layer in a large shallow pan. Brown in 425° oven for 20 to 30 mins; drain off fat. Combine all remaining ingredients, except salt & pepper, in a sauce pan; stir smooth. Cook over medium heat until thick and glossy, stirring constantly. Sprinkle salt and pepper over browned ribs; spoon sweet-sour sauce over each piece, using half the sauce. Reduce oven heat to 350° and bake for 45 minutes. Turn ribs; cover with remaining sauce and bake for 30 minutes more, or until well done. Serves 4 as a main dish.

Makes 5 qts
Upward to 6 qts

Homemade Ice Cream

6 Junket tablets dissolved in 1/4 c cold milk

Beat 6 eggs and add 2 2/3 cups sugar Beat again

1 qt & 1 pint half & half

1 qt milk

8 t vanilla → luke warm

Heat all together and add junket mixture

over

pour into container

Mom's Homemade Ice Cream
1 gallon –
1½ c sugar 5 eggs Beat well
¼ t salt 2 T vanilla Add 2 pts
half + half and enough milk
to fill can a good ¾ full
stir + freeze

ice cream salt – 2 c
ice

Sophie's Best Pumpkin Pie Recipe   1975
1 can pumpkin – 2 eggs – ½ tsp salt
¾ cup sugar – ½ tsp pumpkin pie
spice – 1½ level tbls cornstarch
1⅓ cups milk. Mix and bake –
400° – 15 min – Then 350° – 45 min.

Grandma Hofferber

Mom's Bread Pudding

1½ c milk   ¼ c sugar
1 t vanilla   ¼ t salt
2 eggs   ½ loaf or 4 c Bread cubes
¼ c raisins   (1 T oleo on top)
Cinnamon

Grease 1 qt casserole, set into 1" of water.
Mix ingredients
Drizzle oleo on top
Sprinkle lightly with cinnamon. Bake 350° 55-60 min. or when knife inserted comes out clean
Serve with half & half.
Toast bread cubes a little
Use Lemon Sauce

Oatmeal Bread

1 cup rolled oats
1 cup hot water
2 beaten eggs
1/4 cup sugar
1/4 cup molasses
1 1/4 teas salt
1 1/4 cup oat flour
3 teas B.P
1/4 " soda
1/4 cup chopped raisens or
dates if desired

Place rolled oats in mixing bowl. Add hot water. When cool add beaten eggs, sugar, molasses & salt. Mix well. Add oat flour Baking powder & salt. Put in a 10" loaf pan. Let stand in a warm place 20 min. Bake 350° 45 min. Cover with foil the first 20 min. Then remove.

English Drop Cookie

2 c brown sugar } cream
1 c shortening
add 1 egg beaten
1 c cold coffee
3 c flour   1 t soda   1 t baking powder
1 t cinnamon   3/4 t nutmeg   pinch salt
1 c nuts   1 c raisins

Grandmas Oatmeal Cookies

1 c sugar   2 c oatmeal
3/4 c butter   1 t soda
2 eggs   1 t cinnamon
1/2 c milk   1/4 t salt
2 c flour

cream shortening add sugar & mix
Beat in eggs   add milk & flour
alternately. add oatmeal   drop
by spoon

Mom's Coffee Cake
350° 25 min

1 pk yeast   ½ C warm water
2 t sugar
Combine in lg bowl
scald ½ c milk   ¼ c sugar
    ½ t salt   ¼ t oleo
    stir till cool
add to yeast mixture
add 1 beaten egg   ¼ t cinnamon
3 c flour
Mix - allow to double in size

Roll to ½" thickness
Place in greased 9 x 13 pan
Topping
    ½ c oleo melt till hot
    add 5-6 T flour   add
    ¾ c sugar
    stir till forms balls
Put on top.
Can add drained crushed
pineapple or apple slices

*Walking into Grandma Kohl's home, I would always be overcome with delicious smells. She wore a housedress with an apron, wiped her hands on her apron, and wiped her forehead with a hanky that had been up her sleeve.
That's what I remember.*

grandma kohl's recipes

208 MEAT LOAF

209 PICKLED BEETS

210 RASPBERRY SALAD, CHOCOLATE CAKE

Ann Landers Meat Loaf

2 lbs gr round steak
2 eggs
1½ C. bread crumbs
¾ C. Catsup
1 t. accent
½ C. ~~warm~~ warm Water
1 pkg onion soup mix

Beat thouroughly. Put in loaf pan; cover with 2 strips bacon. Pour over all one eight-ounce can ~~tomato~~ juice

Bake one hour at 350°. Serves six

Pickled Beets (Chinese Recipe)

3 cans of beets   #303 cans
1 c. sugar
2 level teaspoons Cornstarch
1 c. vinegar
24 whole cloves
3 T. Catsup
3 T. Cooking oil
Dash of salt
1 t. vanilla
1½ c. of beet juice

Using a large shallow pan, dump in the sugar and Cornstarch & stir, Mixing well. Add vinegar, cloves, Catsup, oil, salt & vanilla. Stir again well.

Open beets & add 1½ c. juice. Discard the rest. Cut all the beets into bite size & dump in pan.

Cook over medium fire three minutes, stirring all the time until it thickens.

Raspberry Salad

1 pg raspberry jello
1 cup of hot water
1 cup of vanilla ice cream
½ cup chopped pecans —
1 9 oz can of crushed pineapple —

Combine jello with hot water & add ice cream & stir until thoroughly dissolved. Combine undrained pineapple & nuts & 1 diced banana. Add to jello mixture and set in refrig.

Chocolate Cake

1 cup sugar — 2 tbls cocoa —
2 eggs + shortening size of an egg. ½ cup sour milk & a scant teaspoon of soda — mixed in milk — 1 cup of all purpose flour last add ½ cup of hot water. Batter will be thin — cook 425°—

One of Grandma Kohl's hallmarks was that she often wrote multiple recipes on the same sheet of paper. She didn't like to be wasteful.

index

A

African dishes
    Moroccan Chicken Stew over Jumbo Couscous, 99

Appetizers
    Cajun Appetizer Meatballs with Andouille Sausage, 23
    Creamy Crab Rangoon Dip with Baked Won-Ton Chips, 24
    Curried Coconut Chicken Wings, 25
    Deviled Eggs Italia, 26
    Grilled Side of Fresh Salmon with Mustard Dill Glaze, 27
    Luscious Crab Cakes with Remoulade Sauce, 30
    Peanut Chicken Satay, 31
    Pork Potstickers, 28
    Rustic Italian Turkey Meatballs, 29
    Spinach Artichoke Dip, 22

Apples, juice, and cider
    Apple Crisp, 149
    Apple Sage Stuffing, 136
    Apple Walnut Bacon Stuffing, 137
    Caramel Apple Bread Pudding with Brandy Butter, 156
    Cider Herb Salmon Fillet over Black & Orange Rice, 126
    Cider Sauce, 138
    Fall Apple & Walnut Salad with Maple Balsamic Vinaigrette, 49
    Roasted Apple & Butternut Squash Bisque, 57
    Rustic Apple Galette, 162

Apricots
    Leek, Fennel & Apricot Risotto, 90
    Seared Scallops atop Squash & Apricot Risotto, 85

Artichokes
    Chicken & Shrimp Paella, 80
    Deviled Eggs Italia, 26
    Italian Sausage & Arugula Pasta, 91
    Spanish Saffron Chorizo Paella, 81
    Spinach Artichoke Dip, 22
    Stuffed & Baked Tilapia Draped in a Lemon Mornay Sauce, 124

Asian dishes
    Bok Choy (Beef & Pea Pods), 175
    Creamy Crab Rangoon Dip with Baked Won-Ton Chips, 24
    Oriental Pepper Steak, 182
    Peanut Chicken Satay, 31
    Peanut Sauce, 142
    Pork Potstickers, 28
    Sukiyaki, 172
    Sweet & Sour Chicken, Pork or Shrimp, 178–79
    Sweet & Sour Chicken or Pork, 107
    Sweet and Sour Sauce, 24
    Thai "Drunken Noodles" with Plump Shrimp, 92

Asparagus
    Steak Oscar with Béarnaise, 112
    Summertime Fresh Asparagus Quiche, 19

Avocados
    Peach Salsa, 144
    Zesty Lime, Pineapple & Avocado with Baby Greens, 50

B

Bacon
    Apple Sage Stuffing, 136
    Apple Walnut Bacon Stuffing, 137
    Bacon Lentil Soup, 54
    Braised Brussels Sprouts with Bacon, 67
    Creamy Corn & Bacon Chowder, 58
    5 Decker Dinner, 173
    Maple Bacon Wrapped Pork Tenderloin with Rosemary Cherry Sauce, 106
    Orzo Pasta with Bacon, Olives & Feta, 93
    Salad Lyonnaise & Poached Egg, 42
    Sassy Charred Corn Chowder, 63
    Shrimp and Crispy Bacon over Cheesy Grits, 127
    Soul Soothing Loaded Baked Potato Soup, 60
    Spinach & Herb Salad, 43
    Warm Roasted Sweet Potato Maple Bacon Salad, 45

Bananas
    Chef Terrie's Famous Flambéed Bananas Foster with Ice Cream, 148

Beans and legumes. *See also* Sprouts
    Bacon Lentil Soup, 54
    Hearty Black Bean Gumbo, 73
    Italian Bean Salad with Curly Endive, 36
    Moroccan Chicken Stew over Jumbo Couscous, 99
    3 Bean Salad, 171

Beef dishes
    Beef International, 174
    Beef Tenderloin with Jazzy Red Pepper Sauce, 117

Bok Choy (Beef & Pea Pods), 175
Cajun Appetizer Meatballs with Andouille
    Sausage, 23
Chianti Bolognese alla Pappardelle, 86
Coffee Crusted Tenderloin with Red Wine Jus,
    115
Espresso and Chili Rubbed Flank Steak, 109
5 Decker Dinner, 173
Meat Loaf, 208
Oriental Pepper Steak, 182
Out of This World Beef Tenderloin Eggs
    Benedict, 18
Prime Rib, 183
Steak Oscar with Béarnaise, 112
Stir Fried Beef & Pepper Steak, 184
Stuffed Beef Tournedo with Merlot Mustard
    Sauce, 105
Stuffed Cabbage Rolls, 170
Sukiyaki, 172

Beets
    Pickled Beets, 209
    Roasted Beet Salad, 40
    Rosemary Roasted Root Vegetable Salad, 41
Bell peppers. See Peppers
Berries
    Cremini & Leek Risotto with Blueberries, 82
    Festive Quinoa Salad, 47
    Italian Lemon Cake with Rosemary and Golden
        Raisins, 159
    Pear & Walnut Salad, 38
    Raspberry Salad, 210
    Strawberry Margarita Tiramisu, 161
    Strawberry Risotto with Basil Chiffonade, 95
Bok choy
    Bok Choy (Beef & Pea Pods), 175
    Crispy Cod Market Salad, 48
Breads and bread dishes
    Bread Pudding, 202
    Caramel Apple Bread Pudding with Brandy
        Butter, 156
    Crouton Hearts, 61
    Croutons, 35
    Market Bakery Bread, 77
    Mediterranean Salad in an Oven Pancake, 37
    Monkey Bread, 192
    Oatmeal Bread, 203
    Out of This World Beef Tenderloin Eggs
        Benedict, 18
Breakfasts
    Out of This World Beef Tenderloin Eggs
        Benedict, 18
    Summertime Fresh Asparagus Quiche, 19
Brussels sprouts
    Braised Brussels Sprouts with Bacon, 67
Butternut squash. See Squash

Butters
    Brandy Butter, 156
    Whiskey Butter, 135

C

Cabbage
    Crispy Cod Market Salad, 48
    Sauerkraut Salad, 169
    Stuffed Cabbage Rolls, 170
Cakes
    Basil Lime Pound Cake, 157
    Carrot Cake with Cream Cheese Frosting, 151
    Chocolate Cake, 210
    Coffee Cake, 205
    Daffodil Cake, 186
    Grilled Peaches & Angel Food Cake with
        Toasted Almonds, 154
    Italian Lemon Cake with Rosemary and Golden
        Raisins, 159
    Red Velvet Cupcakes, 189
    Red Waldorf Cake, 190
    Sock It to Me Cake, 187
Cannoli
    Chocolate Dipped Cannoli with Pistachio Nuts,
        150
Carrots
    Butternut Squash & Root Vegetable Lasagna,
        94
    Carrot Cake with Cream Cheese Frosting, 151
    Roasted Red Pepper Bisque with Crouton
        Hearts, 61
    Rosemary Roasted Root Vegetable Salad, 41
Casseroles
    Chicken Delight Casserole, 176
Celery
    Baked Rice Pilaf, 66
    Sauerkraut Salad, 169
Cherries
    Romantic Duet of Chicken in Port Cherry Sauce,
        118
Chèvre. See Goat cheese
Chicken dishes
    Andouille & Chicken Jambalaya, 100
    Chicken & Shrimp Paella, 80
    Chicken Cacciatore, 104
    Chicken Delight Casserole, 176
    Chicken Marsala, 110
    Chicken Piccata with Lemon Caper Sauce, 114
    Chicken Rollatini, 116
    Curried Coconut Chicken Wings, 25
    Moroccan Chicken Stew over Jumbo Couscous,
        99

Chicken dishes *(cont.)*
    Peanut Chicken Satay, 31
    Provencal Chicken Breasts with Herbes de Provence Orzo, 113
    Romantic Duet of Chicken in Port Cherry Sauce, 118
    Southwestern Marguerita Chicken Skewers, 102
    Stuffed Pasta Shells, 89
    Sweet & Sour Chicken, Pork or Shrimp, 107, 178–79
    Tomato Vodka Chicken Spaghetti, 84
    Tuscan Chicken Spiedini with Amogio Sauce, 108

Chocolate
    Armstrong German Chocolate Pie, 188
    Bailey's Irish Chocolate Mousse in a Chocolate Cup, 152
    Chocolate Cake, 210
    Chocolate Dipped Cannoli with Pistachio Nuts, 150
    Red Velvet Cupcakes, 189

Citrus dishes and drinks
    Basil Lime Pound Cake, 157
    Chicken Cacciatore, 104
    Chicken Piccata with Lemon Caper Sauce, 114
    Festive Quinoa Salad, 47
    Homemade Caesar & Croutons, 35
    Italian Lemon Cake with Rosemary and Golden Raisins, 159
    Lavender Lemonade, 164
    Lemon Mornay Sauce, 145
    Southwestern Marguerita Chicken Skewers, 102
    Stuffed & Baked Tilapia Draped in a Lemon Mornay Sauce, 124
    Summer Slush, 185
    Sweet and Sour Sauce, 24
    Zesty Lime, Pineapple & Avocado with Baby Greens, 50

Coconut
    Curried Coconut Chicken Wings, 25
    Peanut Chicken Satay, 31
    Peanut Sauce, 142

Coffee and coffee flavor
    Coffee Crusted Tenderloin with Red Wine Jus, 115
    Espresso and Chili Rubbed Flank Steak, 109

Cookies
    Date Pinwheels, 198
    English Drop Cookies, 204
    Lavender Shortbread Cookies, 160
    Oatmeal Cookies, 204

Corn and cornmeal
    Cornbread Stuffed Roasted Turkey Breast with Cider Sauce, 103
    Creamy Corn & Bacon Chowder, 58
    Creamy Polenta with Roasted Corn & Sweet Red Peppers, 68
    Iowa Charred Corn & Jalapeño Risotto, 87
    Popcorn Balls, 191
    Sassy Charred Corn Chowder, 63
    Shrimp and Crispy Bacon over Cheesy Grits, 127
    Sweet Corn Crème Brûlée, 163

Couscous
    Moroccan Chicken Stew over Jumbo Couscous, 99

Cranberries
    Festive Quinoa Salad, 47
    Pear & Walnut Salad, 38

Crème brûlées
    Gingersnap Pumpkin Custard Brûlée, 158
    Sweet Corn Crème Brûlée, 163

Cucumbers
    Cinnamon Pickles, 196
    Cucumber Mint Sauce, 101
    Mostaccioli Noodle Salad, 168
    White Gazpacho, 62

D

Desserts
    Apple Crisp, 149
    Armstrong German Chocolate Pie, 188
    Bailey's Irish Chocolate Mousse in a Chocolate Cup, 152
    Basil Lime Pound Cake, 157
    Bread Pudding, 202
    Caramel Apple Bread Pudding with Brandy Butter, 156
    Carrot Cake with Cream Cheese Frosting, 151
    Chef Terrie's Famous Flambéed Bananas Foster with Ice Cream, 148
    Chocolate Cake, 210
    Chocolate Dipped Cannoli with Pistachio Nuts, 150
    Coffee Cake, 205
    Daffodil Cake, 186
    Date Pinwheels, 198
    English Drop Cookies, 204
    "Fried" Ice Cream, 153
    Gingersnap Pumpkin Custard Brûlée, 158
    Grilled Peaches & Angel Food Cake with Toasted Almonds, 154
    Holiday Pumpkin Tiramisu, 155
    Homemade Ice Cream, 200–201
    Italian Lemon Cake with Rosemary and Golden Raisins, 159
    Lavender Shortbread Cookies, 160
    Monkey Bread, 192

Oatmeal Cookies, 204
Pecan Pie, 191
Popcorn Balls, 191
Pumpkin Pie, 201
Raspberry Salad, 210
Red Velvet Cupcakes, 189
Red Waldorf Cake, 190
Rhubarb Pie, 186
Rustic Apple Galette, 162
Sock It to Me Cake, 187
Strawberry Margarita Tiramisu, 161
Sweet Corn Crème Brûlée, 163

Dips. See Sauces, dips and spreads

Dressings. See also Sauces, dips and spreads
Classic Caesar Dressing, 35
Maple Balsamic Vinaigrette, 49
Tangy Sherry Dressing, 75
Vinaigrette, 41

Drinks
Lavender Lemonade, 164
Summer Slush, 185

E

Egg dishes
Deviled Eggs Italia, 26
Hollandaise Sauce, 132
Out of This World Beef Tenderloin Eggs Benedict, 18
Salad Lyonnaise & Poached Egg, 42
Spinach & Herb Salad, 43
Summertime Fresh Asparagus Quiche, 19

F

Fennel
Chicken Cacciatore, 104
Italian Bean Salad with Curly Endive, 36
Leek, Fennel & Apricot Risotto, 90

Fish and seafood dishes
Baked Salmon en Papillote, 122
Chicken & Shrimp Paella, 80
Chow Har Lock, 177–78
Cider Herb Salmon Fillet over Black & Orange Rice, 126
Clam Linguine, 180
Clam-Mushroom Linguine, 181
Creamy Crab Rangoon Dip with Baked Won-Ton Chips, 24
Crispy Cod Market Salad, 48
Crispy Sea Scallops on Black Rice with Chili Garlic Sauce, 123
Greek Shrimp Pasta, 83
Grilled Halibut, 128
Grilled Side of Fresh Salmon with Mustard Dill Glaze, 27
Lobster Mac & Cheese, 70
Luscious Crab Cakes with Remoulade Sauce, 30
Orange Roughy alla Puttanesca Sauce, 125
Seared Scallops atop Squash & Apricot Risotto, 85
Shrimp and Crispy Bacon over Cheesy Grits, 127
Steak Oscar with Béarnaise, 112
Stuffed & Baked Tilapia Draped in a Lemon Mornay Sauce, 124
Sweet & Sour Chicken, Pork or Shrimp, 178–79
Thai "Drunken Noodles" with Plump Shrimp, 92

French dishes
Baked Salmon en Papillote, 122
French Pork Medallions with Lavender & Grapes, 111
Hollandaise Sauce, 132
Provencal Chicken Breasts with Herbes de Provence Orzo, 113
Salad Lyonnaise & Poached Egg, 42
Steak Oscar with Béarnaise, 112

Frostings
Cream Cheese Frosting for Carrot Cake, 151
Glaze for Italian Lemon Cake, 159

Fruit dishes. See specific fruits

G

Gnocchi
Roasted Butternut Squash & Sage Gnocchi, 71

Goat cheese
Arugula with Goat Cheese Medallions, 39
Crisp Greens with Watermelon, 34
Greek Shrimp Pasta, 83
Mediterranean Salad in an Oven Pancake, 37
Orzo Pasta with Bacon, Olives & Feta, 93
Pear & Walnut Salad, 38
Sprightly Salad of Watercress & Pecan Chèvre Medallions, 44

Grandma Hofferber's recipes
Bread Pudding, 202
Cinnamon Pickles, 196
Coffee Cake, 205
Date Pinwheels, 198
English Drop Cookies, 204
Homemade Ice Cream, 200–201
Oatmeal Bread, 203
Oatmeal Cookies, 204
Pumpkin Pie, 201
Sweet Sour Spareribs, 199
Watermelon Pickles, 197

Grandma Kohl's recipes
    Chocolate Cake, 210
    Meat Loaf, 208
    Pickled Beets, 209
    Raspberry Salad, 210

Grapes
    Champagne Mustard Cream Sauce, 134
    French Pork Medallions with Lavender & Grapes, 111
    White Gazpacho, 62

Green beans
    3 Bean Salad, 171

Greens. *See also* Salads
    Greek Shrimp Pasta, 83
    Grilled Romaine Hearts with Tangy Sherry Dressing, 75
    Italian Sausage & Arugula Pasta, 91
    Orzo Pasta with Bacon, Olives & Feta, 93
    "pre-washed" greens, 33

H

Herbs
    Apple Sage Stuffing, 136
    Basil Lime Pound Cake, 157
    Cider Herb Salmon Fillet over Black & Orange Rice, 126
    Cucumber Mint Sauce, 101
    French Pork Medallions with Lavender & Grapes, 111
    fresh herbs, preserving, 43
    Italian Lemon Cake with Rosemary and Golden Raisins, 159
    Lavender Lemonade, 164
    Lavender Shortbread Cookies, 160
    Poblano Pesto, 141
    Provencal Chicken Breasts with Herbes de Provence Orzo, 113
    Roasted Butternut Squash & Sage Gnocchi, 71
    Rosemary Roasted Root Vegetable Salad, 41
    Spinach & Herb Salad, 43
    Spinach Pesto, 133
    Strawberry Risotto with Basil Chiffonade, 95
    Stuffed Pasta Shells, 89
    Thai "Drunken Noodles" with Plump Shrimp, 92

I

Ice cream
    Chef Terrie's Famous Flambéed Bananas Foster with Ice Cream, 148
    "Fried" Ice Cream, 153
    Homemade Ice Cream, 200–201
    Raspberry Salad, 210

Indian dishes
    Curried Coconut Chicken Wings, 25

Iowa dishes
    Iowa Charred Corn & Jalapeño Risotto, 87
    Stuffed Iowa Pork Chops, 98

Italian dishes
    Autumn Pasta with Butternut Squash Prosciutto Sauce, 88
    Butternut Squash & Root Vegetable Lasagna, 94
    Chianti Bolognese alla Pappardelle, 86
    Chicken Cacciatore, 104
    Chicken Marsala, 110
    Chicken Piccata with Lemon Caper Sauce, 114
    Chicken Rollatini, 116
    Chocolate Dipped Cannoli with Pistachio Nuts, 150
    Cremini & Leek Risotto with Blueberries, 82
    Deviled Eggs Italia, 26
    Eggplant Parmesan, 69
    Holiday Pumpkin Tiramisu, 155
    Italian Bean Salad with Curly Endive, 36
    Italian Lemon Cake with Rosemary and Golden Raisins, 159
    Italian "Love Apple" Soup with Spinach Pesto, 56
    Italian Sausage & Arugula Pasta, 91
    Leek, Fennel & Apricot Risotto, 90
    Mostaccioli Noodle Salad, 168
    Orange Roughy alla Puttanesca Sauce, 125
    Orzo Pasta with Bacon, Olives & Feta, 93
    Rustic Italian Turkey Meatballs, 29
    Seared Scallops atop Squash & Apricot Risotto, 85
    Strawberry Margarita Tiramisu, 161
    Strawberry Risotto with Basil Chiffonade, 95
    Stuffed Pasta Shells, 89
    Tuscan Chicken Spiedini with Amogio Sauce, 108

J

Jalapeño peppers
    Beef Tenderloin with Jazzy Red Pepper Sauce, 117
    Iowa Charred Corn & Jalapeño Risotto, 87
    Peach Salsa, 144
    Tomatillo Sauce, 140

Jello
    Raspberry Salad, 210

Jicama
- Crispy Cod Market Salad, 48

L

Lamb dishes
- Spiced Rubbed Lamb Chops with Cucumber Mint Sauce, 101

Leeks
- Baked Rice Pilaf, 66
- Cremini & Leek Risotto with Blueberries, 82
- Leek, Fennel & Apricot Risotto, 90
- Provencal Chicken Breasts with Herbes de Provence Orzo, 113

Legumes. *See* Beans and legumes

Lemons
- Chicken Cacciatore, 104
- Chicken Piccata with Lemon Caper Sauce, 114
- Homemade Caesar & Croutons, 35
- Italian Lemon Cake with Rosemary and Golden Raisins, 159
- Lavender Lemonade, 164
- Lemon Mornay Sauce, 145
- Summer Slush, 185

Lentils. *See* Beans and legumes

Lettuce. *See* Greens; Salads

Limes
- Basil Lime Pound Cake, 157
- Zesty Lime, Pineapple & Avocado with Baby Greens, 50

M

Maple syrup and flavor
- Fall Apple & Walnut Salad with Maple Balsamic Vinaigrette, 49
- Maple Bacon Wrapped Pork Tenderloin with Rosemary Cherry Sauce, 106
- Warm Roasted Sweet Potato Maple Bacon Salad, 45

Marshmallows
- Popcorn Balls, 191

Meatballs
- Cajun Appetizer Meatballs with Andouille Sausage, 23
- Rustic Italian Turkey Meatballs, 29

Meat main dishes. *See also specific types of meat*
- Andouille & Chicken Jambalaya, 100
- Beef International, 174
- Beef Tenderloin with Jazzy Red Pepper Sauce, 117
- Bok Choy (Beef & Pea Pods), 175
- Chicken Cacciatore, 104
- Chicken Delight Casserole, 176
- Chicken Marsala, 110
- Chicken Piccata with Lemon Caper Sauce, 114
- Chicken Rollatini, 116
- Coffee Crusted Tenderloin with Red Wine Jus, 115
- Cornbread Stuffed Roasted Turkey Breast with Cider Sauce, 103
- Espresso and Chili Rubbed Flank Steak, 109
- 5 Decker Dinner, 173
- French Pork Medallions with Lavender & Grapes, 111
- Maple Bacon Wrapped Pork Tenderloin with Rosemary Cherry Sauce, 106
- Meat Loaf, 208
- Moroccan Chicken Stew over Jumbo Couscous, 99
- Oriental Pepper Steak, 182
- Prime Rib, 183
- Provencal Chicken Breasts with Herbes de Provence Orzo, 113
- Romantic Duet of Chicken in Port Cherry Sauce, 118
- Southwestern Marguerita Chicken Skewers, 102
- Spiced Rubbed Lamb Chops with Cucumber Mint Sauce, 101
- Steak Oscar with Béarnaise, 112
- Stir Fried Beef & Pepper Steak, 184
- Stuffed Beef Tournedo with Merlot Mustard Sauce, 105
- Stuffed Iowa Pork Chops, 98
- Sukiyaki, 172
- Sweet & Sour Chicken, Pork or Shrimp, 107, 178–179
- Tuscan Chicken Spiedini with Amogio Sauce, 108

Mediterranean dishes. *See also* Italian dishes
- Greek Shrimp Pasta, 83
- Mediterranean Salad in an Oven Pancake, 37
- Spiced Rubbed Lamb Chops with Cucumber Mint Sauce, 101

Mexican dishes
- "Fried" Ice Cream, 153
- Poblano Pesto, 141
- Spanish Saffron Chorizo Paella, 81

Mom's recipes
- Armstrong German Chocolate Pie, 188
- Beef International, 174
- Bok Choy (Beef & Pea Pods), 175
- Chicken Delight Casserole, 176
- Chow Har Lock, 177–78
- Clam Linguine, 180

Mom's recipes *(cont.)*
    Clam-Mushroom Linguine, 181
    Daffodil Cake, 186
    5 Decker Dinner, 173
    Monkey Bread, 192
    Mostaccioli Noodle Salad, 168
    Oriental Pepper Steak, 182
    Pecan Pie, 191
    Popcorn Balls, 191
    Prime Rib, 183
    Red Velvet Cupcakes, 189
    Red Waldorf Cake, 190
    Rhubarb Pie, 186
    Sauerkraut Salad, 169
    Sock It to Me Cake, 187
    Stir Fried Beef & Pepper Steak, 184
    Stuffed Cabbage Rolls, 170
    Sukiyaki, 172
    Summer Slush, 185
    Sweet & Sour Chicken, Pork or Shrimp, 178–79
    3 Bean Salad, 171
Mousse
    Bailey's Irish Chocolate Mousse in a Chocolate Cup, 152
Mushrooms
    Bok Choy (Beef & Pea Pods), 175
    Chicken Marsala, 110
    Clam-Mushroom Linguine, 181
    Cremini & Leek Risotto with Blueberries, 82
    Cremini Mushroom Sherry Bisque, 55
    Roasted Butternut Squash & Sage Gnocchi, 71
    Sukiyaki, 172
    Tomato Vodka Chicken Spaghetti, 84

N
Nectarines
    Prosciutto & Nectarine Salad, 46
New Orleans dishes
    Andouille & Chicken Jambalaya, 100
    Cajun Appetizer Meatballs with Andouille Sausage, 23
    Chef Terrie's Famous Flambéed Bananas Foster with Ice Cream, 148
    Hearty Black Bean Gumbo, 73
Nuts
    Apple Walnut Bacon Stuffing, 137
    Arugula with Goat Cheese Medallions, 39
    Carrot Cake with Cream Cheese Frosting, 151
    Chocolate Dipped Cannoli with Pistachio Nuts, 150
    Fall Apple & Walnut Salad with Maple Balsamic Vinaigrette, 49
    Festive Quinoa Salad, 47
    Grilled Peaches & Angel Food Cake with Toasted Almonds, 154
    Peanut Chicken Satay, 31
    Peanut Sauce, 142
    Pear & Walnut Salad, 38
    Pecan Pie, 191
    Sprightly Salad of Watercress & Pecan Chèvre Medallions, 44
    Thai "Drunken Noodles" with Plump Shrimp, 92
    White Gazpacho, 62

O
Oats
    Apple Crisp, 149
    Oatmeal Bread, 203
    Oatmeal Cookies, 204
Okra
    Andouille & Chicken Jambalaya, 100
    Hearty Black Bean Gumbo, 73
Olives
    Chicken Cacciatore, 104
    Eggplant Parmesan, 69
    Italian Sausage & Arugula Pasta, 91
    Mediterranean Salad in an Oven Pancake, 37
    Orange Roughy alla Puttanesca Sauce, 125
    Orzo Pasta with Bacon, Olives & Feta, 93
    Provencal Chicken Breasts with Herbes de Provence Orzo, 113
    Rustic Italian Turkey Meatballs, 29
    Stuffed & Baked Tilapia Draped in a Lemon Mornay Sauce, 124
    Stuffed Pasta Shells, 89
Orange juice
    Summer Slush, 185

P
Pasta dishes. *See also* Couscous
    Autumn Pasta with Butternut Squash Prosciutto Sauce, 88
    Butternut Squash & Root Vegetable Lasagna, 94
    Chianti Bolognese alla Pappardelle, 86
    Clam Linguine, 180
    Clam-Mushroom Linguine, 181
    Greek Shrimp Pasta, 83
    Italian Sausage & Arugula Pasta, 91
    Lobster Mac & Cheese, 70
    Mostaccioli Noodle Salad, 168

Orzo Pasta with Bacon, Olives & Feta, 93
Provencal Chicken Breasts with Herbes de Provence Orzo, 113
Stuffed Pasta Shells, 89
Thai "Drunken Noodles" with Plump Shrimp, 92
Tomato Vodka Chicken Spaghetti, 84

Peaches
   Grilled Peaches & Angel Food Cake with Toasted Almonds, 154
   Peach Salsa, 144

Peas
   Baked Rice Pilaf, 66
   Bok Choy (Beef & Pea Pods), 175
   Chicken & Shrimp Paella, 80
   Oriental Pepper Steak, 182
   Spinach & Herb Salad, 43

Peppers
   Beef International, 174
   Beef Tenderloin with Jazzy Red Pepper Sauce, 117
   Chicken & Shrimp Paella, 80
   Chicken Cacciatore, 104
   Creamy Corn & Bacon Chowder, 58
   Creamy Polenta with Roasted Corn & Sweet Red Peppers, 68
   Hearty Black Bean Gumbo, 73
   Iowa Charred Corn & Jalapeño Risotto, 87
   Moroccan Chicken Stew over Jumbo Couscous, 99
   Mostaccioli Noodle Salad, 168
   Out of This World Beef Tenderloin Eggs Benedict, 18
   Poblano Pesto, 141
   Roasted Red Pepper Bisque with Crouton Hearts, 61
   Sauerkraut Salad, 169
   Stir Fried Beef & Pepper Steak, 184
   Stuffed & Baked Tilapia Draped in a Lemon Mornay Sauce, 124
   Sweet & Sour Chicken, Pork or Shrimp, 178–79
   Sweet & Sour Chicken or Pork, 107
   Thai "Drunken Noodles" with Plump Shrimp, 92
   3 Bean Salad, 171
   Tomatillo Sauce, 140

Pickles
   Cinnamon Pickles, 196
   Pickled Beets, 209
   Watermelon Pickles, 197

Pies
   Armstrong German Chocolate Pie, 188
   Pecan Pie, 191
   Pumpkin Pie, 201
   Rhubarb Pie, 186

Pineapple
   Carrot Cake with Cream Cheese Frosting, 151
   Raspberry Salad, 210
   Sweet & Sour Chicken, Pork or Shrimp, 178–79
   Sweet & Sour Chicken or Pork, 107
   Sweet Sour Spareribs, 199
   Zesty Lime, Pineapple & Avocado with Baby Greens, 50

Polenta
   Creamy Polenta with Roasted Corn & Sweet Red Peppers, 68

Pomegranate
   Arugula with Goat Cheese Medallions, 39

Pork dishes. *See also* Bacon; Sausage dishes
   Autumn Pasta with Butternut Squash Prosciutto Sauce, 88
   Chianti Bolognese alla Pappardelle, 86
   French Pork Medallions with Lavender & Grapes, 111
   Maple Bacon Wrapped Pork Tenderloin with Rosemary Cherry Sauce, 106
   Pork Potstickers, 28
   Prosciutto & Nectarine Salad, 46
   Stuffed Iowa Pork Chops, 98
   Sweet & Sour Chicken, Pork or Shrimp, 178–79
   Sweet & Sour Chicken or Pork, 107
   Sweet Sour Spareribs, 199

Potatoes. *See also* Sweet potatoes
   Creamy Corn & Bacon Chowder, 58
   Garlic Smashed Potatoes, 72
   Rosemary Roasted Root Vegetable Salad, 41
   Soul Soothing Loaded Baked Potato Soup, 60

Pumpkin. *See* Squash

Q

Quinoa
   Festive Quinoa Salad, 47

R

Raisins
   Italian Lemon Cake with Rosemary and Golden Raisins, 159

Rice dishes
   Andouille & Chicken Jambalaya, 100
   Baked Rice Pilaf, 66
   Chicken & Shrimp Paella, 80
   Cider Herb Salmon Fillet over Black & Orange Rice, 126
   Cremini & Leek Risotto with Blueberries, 82

Rice dishes (cont.)
- Crispy Sea Scallops on Black Rice with Chili Garlic Sauce, 123
- Iowa Charred Corn & Jalapeño Risotto, 87
- Leek, Fennel & Apricot Risotto, 90
- Romantic Duet of Chicken in Port Cherry Sauce, 118
- Seared Scallops atop Squash & Apricot Risotto, 85
- Spanish Saffron Chorizo Paella, 81
- Stir Fried Beef & Pepper Steak, 184
- Strawberry Risotto with Basil Chiffonade, 95
- Sweet & Sour Chicken, Pork or Shrimp, 178–79
- Sweet & Sour Chicken or Pork, 107
- Wild Rice Soup with Smoked Sausage, 59

Rum
- Chef Terrie's Famous Flambéed Bananas Foster with Ice Cream, 148
- Summer Slush, 185

S

Salads
- Arugula with Goat Cheese Medallions, 39
- Crisp Greens with Watermelon, 34
- Crispy Cod Market Salad, 48
- Fall Apple & Walnut Salad with Maple Balsamic Vinaigrette, 49
- Festive Quinoa Salad, 47
- Homemade Caesar & Croutons, 35
- Italian Bean Salad with Curly Endive, 36
- Mediterranean Salad in an Oven Pancake, 37
- Mostaccioli Noodle Salad, 168
- Pear & Walnut Salad, 38
- Prosciutto & Nectarine Salad, 46
- Roasted Beet Salad, 40
- Rosemary Roasted Root Vegetable Salad, 41
- Salad Lyonnaise & Poached Egg, 42
- Sauerkraut Salad, 169
- Spinach & Herb Salad, 43
- Sprightly Salad of Watercress & Pecan Chèvre Medallions, 44
- 3 Bean Salad, 171
- Warm Roasted Sweet Potato Maple Bacon Salad, 45
- Zesty Lime, Pineapple & Avocado with Baby Greens, 50

Sauces, dips and spreads. See also Dressings; Frostings; Butters
- Amogio Sauce, for Tuscan Chicken Spiedini, 108
- Apple Sage Stuffing, 136
- Apple Walnut Bacon Stuffing, 137
- Béarnaise, 112
- Champagne Mustard Cream Sauce, 134
- Chili Garlic Sauce, 143
- Cider Sauce, 138
- Creamy Crab Rangoon Dip, 24
- Cucumber Mint Sauce, 101
- Hollandaise Sauce, 132
- Lemon Mornay Sauce, 145
- Peach Salsa, 144
- Peanut Sauce, 142
- Poblano Pesto, 141
- Remoulade Sauce, 30
- Spinach Artichoke Dip, 22
- Spinach Pesto, 133
- Sweet and Sour Sauce, 24
- Tomatillo Sauce, 140
- Whiskey Pepper Cream Sauce, 139

Sausage dishes
- Andouille & Chicken Jambalaya, 100
- Cajun Appetizer Meatballs with Andouille Sausage, 23
- Chicken & Shrimp Paella, 80
- Italian Sausage & Arugula Pasta, 91
- Spanish Saffron Chorizo Paella, 81
- Wild Rice Soup with Smoked Sausage, 59

Seafood dishes. See Fish and seafood dishes

Side dishes
- Baked Rice Pilaf, 66
- Braised Brussels Sprouts with Bacon, 67
- Creamy Polenta with Roasted Corn & Sweet Red Peppers, 68
- Eggplant Parmesan, 69
- Garlic Smashed Potatoes, 72
- Grilled Romaine Hearts with Tangy Sherry Dressing, 75
- Hearty Black Bean Gumbo, 73
- Lobster Mac & Cheese, 70
- Roasted Butternut Squash & Sage Gnocchi, 71
- Spaghetti Squash with Spinach Pesto & Tomato, 74
- Summertime Succotash, 76

Soups
- Bacon Lentil Soup, 54
- Creamy Corn & Bacon Chowder, 58
- Cremini Mushroom Sherry Bisque, 55
- Italian "Love Apple" Soup with Spinach Pesto, 56
- Roasted Apple & Butternut Squash Bisque, 57
- Roasted Red Pepper Bisque with Crouton Hearts, 61
- Sassy Charred Corn Chowder, 63
- Soul Soothing Loaded Baked Potato Soup, 60
- White Gazpacho, 62
- Wild Rice Soup with Smoked Sausage, 59

Spanish dishes
    Chicken & Shrimp Paella, 80
    Spanish Saffron Chorizo Paella, 81
    White Gazpacho, 62
Spinach
    Chicken Rollatini, 116
    Italian "Love Apple" Soup with Spinach Pesto, 56
    Spaghetti Squash with Spinach Pesto & Tomato, 74
    Spinach & Herb Salad, 43
    Spinach Artichoke Dip, 22
    Spinach Pesto, 133
Spreads. *See* Sauces, dips and spreads
Sprouts
    Bok Choy (Beef & Pea Pods), 175
    Crispy Cod Market Salad, 48
    Thai "Drunken Noodles" with Plump Shrimp, 92
Squash
    Autumn Pasta with Butternut Squash Prosciutto Sauce, 88
    Butternut Squash & Root Vegetable Lasagna, 94
    Cider Herb Salmon Fillet over Black & Orange Rice, 126
    Gingersnap Pumpkin Custard Brûlée, 158
    Holiday Pumpkin Tiramisu, 155
    Pumpkin Pie, 201
    Roasted Apple & Butternut Squash Bisque, 57
    Roasted Butternut Squash & Sage Gnocchi, 71
    Seared Scallops atop Squash & Apricot Risotto, 85
    Spaghetti Squash with Spinach Pesto & Tomato, 74
Stuffing
    Apple Sage Stuffing, 136
    Apple Walnut Bacon Stuffing, 137
Sweet potatoes
    Butternut Squash & Root Vegetable Lasagna, 94
    Rosemary Roasted Root Vegetable Salad, 41
    Warm Roasted Sweet Potato Maple Bacon Salad, 45

T

Terrie's tidbits
    on cooking wine, 62
    on fresh herbs, 43
    on leftover wine, 55
    on "pre-washed" greens, 33
    on risotto, 90

Tomatoes
    Chianti Bolognese alla Pappardelle, 86
    Chicken & Shrimp Paella, 80
    Chicken Cacciatore, 104
    Eggplant Parmesan, 69
    Greek Shrimp Pasta, 83
    Italian Bean Salad with Curly Endive, 36
    Italian "Love Apple" Soup with Spinach Pesto, 56
    Italian Sausage & Arugula Pasta, 91
    Mostaccioli Noodle Salad, 168
    Orange Roughy alla Puttanesca Sauce, 125
    Peach Salsa, 144
    Provencal Chicken Breasts with Herbes de Provence Orzo, 113
    Rustic Italian Turkey Meatballs, 29
    Spaghetti Squash with Spinach Pesto & Tomato, 74
    Spanish Saffron Chorizo Paella, 81
    Stuffed Cabbage Rolls, 170
    Stuffed Pasta Shells, 89
    Sweet & Sour Chicken, Pork or Shrimp, 178–79
    Sweet & Sour Chicken or Pork, 107
    Thai "Drunken Noodles" with Plump Shrimp, 92
    Tomato Vodka Chicken Spaghetti, 84
Turkey dishes
    Cornbread Stuffed Roasted Turkey Breast with Cider Sauce, 103
    Rustic Italian Turkey Meatballs, 29

V

Vegetable dishes. *See also specific vegetables*
    Baked Salmon en Papillote, 122
    Butternut Squash & Root Vegetable Lasagna, 94
    Summertime Succotash, 76

W

Watermelon
    Crisp Greens with Watermelon, 34
    Watermelon Pickles, 197
Wine
    Autumn Pasta with Butternut Squash Prosciutto Sauce, 88
    Champagne Mustard Cream Sauce, 134
    Chianti Bolognese alla Pappardelle, 86
    Chicken Marsala, 110
    Cider Sauce, 138

Coffee Crusted Tenderloin with Red Wine Jus, 115
for cooking, 62
Cremini Mushroom Sherry Bisque, 55
leftover, 55
Romantic Duet of Chicken in Port Cherry Sauce, 118
Seared Scallops atop Squash & Apricot Risotto, 85
Strawberry Risotto with Basil Chiffonade, 95
Stuffed Beef Tournedo with Merlot Mustard Sauce, 105

Won-ton wrappers
    Creamy Crab Rangoon Dip with Baked Won-Ton Chips, 24
    Pork Potstickers, 28

www.ingramcontent.com/pod-product-compliance
Lightning Source LLC
Chambersburg PA
CBHW080458240426
43673CB00005B/227